how2become

HOW TO JOIN
THE RAF RESERVES

www.How2Become.com

Orders: Please contact How2become Ltd, Suite 2, 50 Churchill Square Business Centre, Kings Hill, Kent ME19 4YU.

You can order through Amazon.co.uk under ISBN 978-1-910602-45-4, via the website www.How2Become.com or through Gardners.com.

ISBN: 978-1-910602-45-4

First published in 2015 by How2become Ltd.

Typeset for How2become Ltd by Anton Pshinka.

Disclaimer

Every effort has been made to ensure that the information contained within this guide is accurate at the time of publication. How2become Ltd are not responsible for anyone failing any part of any selection process as a result of the information contained within this guide. How2become Ltd and their authors cannot accept any responsibility for any errors or omissions within this guide, however caused. No responsibility for loss or damage occasioned by any person acting, or refraining from action, as a result of the material in this publication can be accepted by How2become Ltd.

The information within this guide does not represent the views of any third party service or organisation.

CONTENTS

INTRODUCTION

I can remember sitting in the Armed Forces careers office at the age of 16, waiting patiently for the interview section of my application to join the Royal Navy. I had already passed the written tests, and despite never having sat an interview in my life, I was confident of success. I had worked very hard studying for the job that I was applying for, and had thoroughly practised my interview technique.

At the end of the interview I was told that I had easily passed, and all that was left to complete was the medical. Unfortunately, I was overweight. I was worried that I might fail. At the medical, my fears became a reality, and I was told by the doctor that I would have to lose a stone in weight before they would accept me. I sat at the bus stop feeling gutted, embarrassed and sorry for myself; wondering what job I was going to apply for next. My dream of joining the Armed Forces was over. I didn't know which way to turn. It was at that particular moment that my life changed forever.

As the bus approached, I began to feel a sense of determination to lose weight, and get fit in the shortest time possible. I remember thinking that there was no time like the present for getting started on my fitness regime. So, instead of getting on the bus, I opted to walk the three miles home. When I got home, I sat in my room and wrote out a three-step 'plan of action' that would dictate how I was going to lose the weight required. The plan looked like this:

1.   Every weekday morning I will get up at 6am and run 3 miles.

2.   Instead of catching the bus to college and back, I will walk.

3.   I will eat healthily and I will not go over the recommended daily calorific intake.

Every day I would read my action plan, and use it as a reminder of what I needed to do. Within a few weeks, I had lost over a stone in weight, and was a lot fitter too. When I returned back to the surgery for my medical, the doctor was amazed that I had managed to lose so much weight in such a short space of time. He was pleased that I had been so determined to pass the medical. Six months later, I started my basic training course with the Royal Navy. Ever since that day, I have always made sure that I do my utmost to prepare properly for any job application. If I do fail a particular interview or section of an application process, then I will always go out of my way to ask for feedback, so that I can improve for next time. I use 'action plans' in just about every element of my work today. Action plans allow you to focus on what you want to achieve. In this guide, I will teach you how you can use your own action plan to achieve your dream job as an RAF Reservist.

Throughout my career, I have always been successful. The reason for this is not because I am better than the next person, but simply because I prepare better. I didn't do well at school, so I have had to work harder to pass the exams and written tests that now form an essential part of most job application processes. Preparation was the key to my success, and now it will be the key to yours. Without the right preparation, you are only setting yourself up to fail. It is hard to join the RAF Reserves, but if you follow the advice given in this guide then you will increase your chances dramatically.

The men and women of the Armed Forces carry out an amazing job. They are there to protect us and our country, and they do this with great pride, passion, professionalism and commitment. They deserve to be congratulated for the job that they do. Before you apply to join the RAF Reserves, you need to be fully confident that you too are capable of providing the same level of skill and determination. If you think you can do it, and believe that you can rise to the challenge, then you might be just the type of person that the RAF is looking for.

CHAPTER 1

RAF Reserve Requirements

A career with the RAF Reserves is one of the best you can get. As an RAF Reserve you will have the opportunity to live your normal life, whilst devoting your spare-time towards the development of key skills and training needed for the RAF. RAF Reserves perform exactly the same activities as full-time employees, with the difference being that they work from local territory on a part-time basis. While you will still take on periods of overseas training, you will only be required to work on a full-time basis for the RAF should they summon you. For example, in the event of a war. While this may seem unlikely, you should only be applying to the RAF Reserves if you are someone who IS prepared to fight for the country, should the RAF require you to do so.

Working for the RAF requires technical expertise that exceeds that of other roles within the Armed Forces. The application process, therefore, is considerably harder in terms of the technical knowledge that is required. Many of the roles and careers within the RAF will require you to possess GCSEs in Maths, English and a Science-based subject. However, there are also a number of career options open to those who have no qualifications at all. Whichever path you choose, you will need to pass aptitude tests, interviews and various health and fitness assessments.

In order to progress through each stage of the RAF selection process, you must prepare fully and put in 100% effort. As I have mentioned, the key to success is preparation. The most common reason for failing the Royal Air Force selection process is lack of preparation. Remember that the smallest things can make the biggest difference. Try to imagine yourself as an RAF careers officer. What would you be looking for in potential applicants? What would stand out? Having the ability to listen to what you are being told is very important. If you are asked to attend an interview or test at a specific time or place, then make sure you turn up on time. Careers in the RAF require people who are extremely punctual. Therefore, creating the right impression is crucial!

Remember, good things in life don't always come easy. As I coach you through the selection process, I want you to promise yourself one thing – you will work hard and will continue to look for ways to improve on your weaker areas. My recipe for success has been exactly that – to work hard and better myself.

With perseverance and determination comes greater success. If you give it your all, there is no reason that you can't achieve anything you want in life.

HOW TO PREPARE FOR THE RAF RESERVES SELECTION PROCESS

Before I explain the different stages of the RAF selection process, it is important for me to explain how you need to go about your preparation. As I have mentioned, the more preparation you do, the better your chances of success will be. Furthermore, it's important to structure your preparation. I previously discussed the idea of using an 'action plan'. This is a great method of structuring your approach. The action plan sets out what you are going to do and when you are going to do it. It's very similar to a shopping list, in the fact that you are writing down exactly what you need to get whilst you are out shopping. Just by writing down the steps that you are going to take, you will be adding invaluable structure and organisation to your approach.

I often write my action plans down in tables, to make them clear and simple to read. Below is an action plan that I would use if I was going through the RAF Reserves selection process right now:

MY ACTION PLAN FOR PREPARING FOR RAF SELECTION – EXAMPLE ONLY

Monday	Tuesday	Wednesday	Thursday	Friday	Saturday	Sunday
60 minutes Airman/ Airwoman Test preparation and 30 minutes reading about RAF history	60 minutes study relating to my choice of career	60 minutes Airman/ Airwoman Test preparation and 30 minutes reading about RAF history	Rest day	60 minute study relating to RAF life, airbases and equipment including my recruitment literature	60 minutes Airman/ Airwoman Test preparation and 30 minutes reading about RAF history	60 minutes study relating to my choice of career in the RAF
30 minute run then I will work on my sit ups and press ups	45 minutes gym work (light weights) including sit ups and press ups	30 minute run or bleep test preparation		1.5 mile run (best effort) and bleep test preparation. Also include some sit ups and press up work	45 minutes gym work (light weights) or 30 minute swim	60 minute study relating to RAF life, airbases and equipment including my recruitment literature

---

The above action plan/timetable would ensure that I focused on the following three key developmental areas:

• Improving my mental and physical fitness in preparation for the RAF health and fitness assessments;

• Improving my ability to carry out the psychometric tests in preparation for the aptitude assessments;

• Improving my knowledge of the RAF Reserves, consequently increasing my chances of passing the interview.

By following a structured training and development programme during your preparation, then you are far more likely to succeed. For every element of the RAF Reserve selection process, use an action plan which sets out exactly what you are going to do, and when.

Now, let's take a look at the selection process in more detail.

THE RAF RESERVE SELECTION PROCESS

The selection process to join the RAF Reserves is as follows:

- Application Form
- Information Day
- Psychometric Tests
- Interviews
- Health Assessment Day
- Fitness Related Tests
- Further Training.

At first glance, this list might seem a little intimidating. However, there is a way that you can pass all of these stages, and secure your dream career. The way to do this is to use the RAF core competencies.

Below, I have broken up the core competencies in order to improve your understanding of what is expected from you, and to increase your chances of being successful.

RAF CORE COMPETENCIES

Core Competencies refer to the key behaviours which you will be expected to demonstrate whilst a) applying for a job position, and b) working within the role. They are an integral part of any job selection process, and are now used by almost every single employer.

In order to successfully attain a position as an RAF Reserve, you will need to show an ability to demonstrate these core competencies at all times and to a high standard.

'Respect for Others':

Respect for others is extremely important in the RAF. Not only do you need to have respect for the country that you are serving, but you need to have respect for your commanding officers, subordinates and fellow RAF personnel.

It's important to have a sense of pride for your role. Remember that it is your duty as an RAF serviceman/woman to put other people first. Having respect for others also means having a good understanding of diversity, and a zero tolerance policy towards discrimination.

Whilst working for the RAF, or anywhere for that matter, you will meet many different people from many different backgrounds. You need to be able to work with these people, respect their differences and build strong professional relationships.

'Self-Respect':

Having self-respect is important. Individuals with self-respect have a great sense of dignity and integrity. In order to perform your role successfully, you need to be able to value your own professional input and attitude towards the work, and your personal life.

Having self-respect means maintaining and adhering to a code of behaviour which won't bring disrepute to your reputation, or to the RAF.

'Integrity':

Integrity is fundamental for RAF personnel. It refers to having the ability to behave in an ethical and respectful manner, and having the courage to do the right thing in all circumstances.

As an RAF serviceman, whether you are a Reserve or full-time, your colleagues need to be able to establish a level of trust and confidence in you. You must have the conviction to take what you believe is the right course of action, regardless of the consequences.

By demonstrating that you are someone who will never compromise their moral integrity, you will earn the respect of the other members of your unit, and build long lasting professional relationships.

'Honesty':

To further your colleagues respect, it is important that you are an honest person. Remember that your colleagues need to be able to rely on you. If they can't trust you, or believe that you are lying, then it will be difficult to work as a coherent team.

At all times, you should avoid being deceitful, dishonest or breaching the confidence of other individuals.

'Responsibility':

RAF personnel have a huge amount of responsibility. Therefore, it's important that they can behave accordingly at all times. Responsibility is not something that individuals can pick and choose, RAF personnel must behave in a responsible manner 100% of the time, regardless of the role that they find themselves in. By behaving in a responsible manner, individuals can ensure that they earn the respect of their superiors, colleagues and subordinates.

Remember that the RAF is a highly esteemed, globally recognised organisation. You must behave in a manner befitting the service.

'Physical Courage':

Physical courage means being able to use deadly force, in order to keep with the responsibilities of the service. If called into action, RAF Reserves must be prepared for the possibility of taking the lives of others, or risking their own. They may be witness to the injury or death of their colleagues. They must be able to continue their duties regardless of what is going on around them. This requires extreme physical courage.

Remember that when you sign up to the RAF, you are committing to defend the interests of the nation at whatever cost, even if that means sacrificing your life.

'Loyalty':

Loyalty is a fundamental quality that all RAF personnel must have. As we have mentioned, from the moment you sign up for the RAF, you commit yourself entirely to defending and protecting the nation. At times, you will need to uphold this commitment under extremely difficult circumstances, therefore your loyalty is paramount.

Loyalty is also one of the key cornerstones of teamwork. Team members need to be loyal in order to establish a level of trust, respect and commitment for the good of the unit.

'Teamwork':

Teamwork is an essential element to working in the RAF. On the large majority of occasions, you will be positioned within a wider unit, and therefore will have to work as part of a team. Not only will you have to work with your unit, but with countless other members of the service too. You will also be expected to work with citizens, the armed forces of other nations and civil servants. You will rely on your team to support you through difficult operations and equally, they will rely on you for your support and expertise.

'Commitment To Excellence':

By signing a commitment to the RAF Reserves, you sign a commitment to excellence. RAF employees need to demonstrate a constant desire to improve existing skills, and learn new skills. This helps to ensure that the RAF remains an elite force.

Remember that excellence is about more than just the skills involved in the job. It's about the way that RAF personnel go about handling tasks, undertaking their responsibilities and performing to the best of their ability, regardless of the conditions that they are working in.

Every single member of the RAF, regardless of rank, has a duty to maintain the highest possible professional standards. Remember that your adherence to excellence has a direct effect on the people you are protecting back at home, so it's vitally important.

'Discipline':

As I'm sure you are aware, discipline is a fundamental part of RAF life. By having good discipline, individuals can achieve things that they might only have dreamed of doing otherwise.

Discipline is rigorously upheld by all members of the RAF, and must be adhered to both on and off-duty. If you are someone who struggles with discipline, or following rules, then it goes without saying that you might be applying for the wrong job. Don't be put off though. As long as you are willing to learn, and don't fight the system, the RAF will teach you discipline and shape you into an outstanding service member.

HOW TO USE THESE COMPETENCIES

So, how can we use these competencies to help you get the job? The answer is simple. Learn them, and then incorporate them into your responses. During the selection process, you will see a large number of questions which require an understanding of the qualities that an RAF Reserve should have. By using the above list, you can put yourself one step ahead of the competition, and show the assessors from a very early stage that you are suitable for the role.

When answering interview, application form and other situational questions, try to incorporate as many of these qualities into your responses as you can. You need to learn how to ascertain which qualities are relevant to which situation, and then give examples of when you have demonstrated those qualities in the past. It's extremely important that you tell the assessors what you did, rather than what you would do or wished you had done. Throughout this guide, we'll give you numerous sample answers that demonstrate how you can break down difficult application, situational and interview questions, and utilise the correct competency to construct your answer.

Once you have passed the interview stage, a decision will be made on whether you have been successful. Following this, you'll have to cement the decision by passing various health, fitness and medical checks, along with partaking in further specialist training. Now, let's take a look at each of the different stages of the selection process in more detail.

CHAPTER 2

*Top 10 Tips
For Success*

Over the next few pages, I have provided you with a number of important tips that I believe will help you to successfully pass the RAF selection process. Many of these tips are simple ones, however the majority of candidates fail to implement them, and end up failing as a result.

Follow each tip carefully, and make sure you implement them into your preparation strategy and action plan:

TIP 1:

Prepare Fully for Every Stage of the Selection Process

As I have already stated at the beginning of this guide, preparation is crucial to your success. Candidates who prepare fully for the selection process will do well. If you don't prepare fully, then there is a strong possibility that you will fail. There are a number of important things that you can do in order to improve your chances of success.

Research

The first important area is your research of the RAF Reserve and the role that you are applying for. During the selection interviews, the RAF will want to see that you have studied their organisation, your choice of career and the training that you will undergo if you are successful. The only way to do this is to sit down and read your recruitment literature, study the RAF website and also to speak to serving members of the RAF. You may also find it useful to learn a little bit about the history of the service. Whilst not essential, this will demonstrate to the assessors that you have gone out of your way to learn as much as possible about the organisation, its success stories and what it stands for.

Action Plan

In an earlier section of the guide, I recommended that you implement some form of action plan into your preparation. This will ensure that your preparation is focused, and targets the right areas. For example, if you have never attended an interview before, then it is wise to carry out a 'mock interview', before you attend the real one. This involves getting a friend or member of your family to sit down and interview you, using the questions that are contained within this guide. The more mock interviews that you take, the better you'll become.

Aptitude Tests

It is also important to work on your ability to pass the aptitude tests. These consist of a number of different psychometric assessments that are designed to assess your ability to carry out tasks quickly and accurately. Within a separate section of this guide, I have provided you with lots of different test questions to help you prepare. I would recommend that you carry out lots of sample test questions over a prolonged period of time, as opposed to 'cramming' the night before. 'Little and often' is the key to improvement, and it is also important to check your answers at the end to ensure that you can improve for next time.

TIP 2:

Practice Plenty of Psychometric Test Questions

The RAF has made brilliant progress in its aptitude testing policies over the years, in particular to the quality and range of the tests it uses. The tests that they use to assess potential candidates are now driven by detailed assessments of training requirements. If you score poorly on the tests, then there is a strong likelihood that you will not be able to perform your role in the RAF competently.

The aptitude tests are multiple choice in nature, and will cover 7 different testing areas. They are designed to assess your ability to carry out tasks quickly and accurately. Your results in the test will determine your suitability for a career in the RAF, so it is very important that you achieve the highest scores possible. You can achieve this through deliberate and repetitive practice. This involves finding out which areas you need to improve on, and then carrying out practice in that area until you become competent.

The Aptitude Tests consist of:

- **A verbal reasoning test:** designed to assess how you use and understand written information;

- **A numerical reasoning test:** assesses your ability to work with numbers and mathematical calculations, such as fractions, formulae, graphs and tables;

- **A spatial reasoning test:** examine your understanding of how shapes and different objects rotate and move;

- **A work rate test:** assesses how quickly you can carry out specific tasks;

- **An electrical comprehension test:** assesses your level of electrical competence;

- **A mechanical comprehension test:** determines how well you understand mechanical concepts;

- **A memory test.**

As you progress through this guide, you will notice that I have included lots of sample test questions that will help you to prepare for the different tests. You will need to set aside plenty of time in the build up to your aptitude tests, in order to practice them. Use the questions within this book to help you prepare. Just by practicing lots of similar tests, your mind will begin to work faster under pressurised conditions. Whilst working through the tests, make sure you check any questions you get wrong. This is a crucial part of your development.

TIP 3:

Create the Right Impression

When you apply to join the RAF Reserves, you will be communicating at times with experienced and professional serving RAF Officers and recruitment staff. They are highly trained to pick out the candidates who they believe are worth investing time and money in, and will be assessing you from the word go. Whenever you make contact with the careers office, either by phone or in person, make sure that you are polite, courteous and go out of your way to create the right impression.

When I was going through the Armed Forces selection process, I would always make an effort to dress smart when attending the careers office. Often, there would always be other applicants at the office who were wearing jeans, tracksuits and trainers. Whilst there is no requirement to dress smart when you attend the careers office, I believe that it will go a long way to helping you impress the recruitment staff.

When you telephone the careers office to obtain an application form, or even just for an informal chat, I strongly advise that you are polite and courteous at all times. General good manners, such as 'good morning' or 'thank you for your time' are not as commonplace in today's society as they used to be. Being polite and courteous when you communicate with the careers officer can help you to create the right impression, right from the start.

Members of the Armed Forces, including those of the RAF, are role models in society. How would you expect a member of the RAF to behave? They would be courteous, respectful and polite, of course, and therefore so should you. Even though you have not yet joined the RAF Reserve, you should still demonstrate your potential at every opportunity.

During my research into this guide, I spoke to many serving officers. One in particular told me that she would be far more impressed if an applicant attended the careers office smartly dressed with polished shoes. Unfortunately, she said, it doesn't happen that often.

TIP 4:

Take Pride in your Appearance

Top Tips

At the end of my initial Armed Forces basic training, I received an award for being the best on my course for 'kit upkeep and bearing'. I'd worked very hard throughout my training, and always ensured that I looked smart and took pride in my appearance. I can remember the Warrant Officer taking us for drills every Friday morning; and at the top of his voice, shouting: 'Shiny shoes, shiny mind!' I used to think that this was a fantastic statement. What he was essentially saying is that if you take pride in your appearance, then your mind will be more positive, and you'll feel better about yourself. If you feel good about yourself, then this will reflect in everything that you do.

How many people do you know that clean their shoes every day? Not many, I'm sure, but this can go a long way to creating the right impression. Walking into the careers office with dirty shoes will not create a good impression, and neither will dirty nails or generally poor personal hygiene. When you join the RAF, you will be living and sleeping with lots of people in the same room. Therefore, personal hygiene is important, and you will need to have an ability to look after yourself and your equipment.

If you're called up for full-time duty with the RAF, or even during training, you will be inspected every day. It is far better to demonstrate to the careers officer that you are a smart and clean individual, who cares about your appearance. Your budget might not be big, but you can purchase a shirt and tie for very little money nowadays. They don't have to be expensive or good quality, but showing that you've made an effort will create the right impression. If you cannot afford to buy a shirt and tie, then you may be able to borrow these items from a friend or relative. It is definitely worth investing time and effort on your appearance, as jeans, t-shirts and trainers are probably not the best options. Treat every visit to the RAF Careers Office as an opportunity to impress. Remember – you only get ONE chance to create a first impression!

TIP 5:

Prepare for the Fitness Test

You might already be physically active and fit, but even so, it is essential you still prepare. During the selection process, you will need to pass the pre-joining fitness test, which consists of a 1.5 mile run in a time of 12 minutes and 12 seconds for men, and 14 minutes and 35 seconds for women. The test will be carried out at either your local Armed Forces Careers Office or alternatively at a gymnasium. At the end of this guide, I have provided you with further details on 'How to get RAF fit', in order to assist you in your preparation.

One of the most effective ways to improve your physical fitness is to embark on a structured running programme. Just by running three miles, three times a week, you will be amazed at how much your fitness and general well-being will improve. Being physically fit means that you will be mentally fit too, and your confidence will increase. I would advise that you aim to better the standard required for the selection process.

When I was going through the selection process for the Armed Forces, I forced myself to get up at 6am every weekday morning, and go for a three mile run. It was tough, especially during the cold mornings, but I soon lost weight and got fit in the process. Getting up at 6am also prepares you for your basic training. After all, you won't be able to lie in bed all morning once your training starts! Keep trying to improve yourself and remember, to be in the RAF you need to be the best that you can be.

TIP 6:

Match the Assessable Qualities

During the RAF selection process you will be assessed against a number of different areas including:

• Your personal turnout and hygiene;

• How physically active and fit you are;

• How well you interact and mix with other people;

• Your ability to work as an effective team member;

• Your levels of maturity and professionalism;

• Your drive and determination to succeed;

• Being self-reliant and responsible;

• How you react to discipline;

• Experience of and reaction to regimentation and routine;

• Your knowledge of the RAF;

• How motivated you are to join the RAF;

• Your personal circumstances.

The above areas will be assessed during your visits to the AFCO and also during the interviews.

Some of the assessable areas are easier to demonstrate than others. For example, your knowledge of the RAF and your chosen career is easy to demonstrate, providing that you put in the effort to learn the information.

Being self-reliant and responsible, however, is a different matter. In order to achieve this, you will need to provide evidence of any responsibilities that you have – either at work, at school or at home. If you have no responsibilities whatsoever, then now is the time to start. Just by taking on weekly household tasks such as cleaning or ironing, you will be demonstrating some form of responsibility at home. If you are currently employed, then ask your manager if it is possible to take on extra responsibility.

Having examples of where you have already met each of the assessable qualities will work heavily in your favour.

TIP 7:

Be a Competent Team Player

During the selection process you will be assessed against your ability to work as an effective team player. Let's take a moment to write down some of the most prominent qualities that an effective team player should possess:

- An ability to interact with, and work with others; regardless of their age, sex, religion, sexual orientation and background;

- Be able to communicate with everyone in the team, and provide the appropriate levels of support and encouragement;

- Be capable of carrying out tasks correctly, professionally and in accordance with guidelines and regulations;

- Being focused on the team's ultimate goal;

- Having a flexible attitude and approach to tasks;

- Putting the needs of the team first, before your own;

- Putting personal differences aside for the sake of the team;

- Being able to listen to other suggestions and contributions.

The RAF prides itself on its ability to operate as an effective team. Try to think of the best football teams in the country. Those that are the most successful are not the ones that have one or two great players, but the ones that have the best players overall. The ability to work as part of a team is essential, and you will be assessed on this during the selection process. Within the RAF Reserves, you will be required to work as part of a team to carry out tasks both large and small.

During the interview, there is a strong possibility that you'll be asked questions that relate to your knowledge of how a team operates, and also your experiences of working in a team to achieve a common task or goal. Before you move on to the next tip, try to think of an occasion when you have worked effectively as part of a team to achieve a goal or task. An example of this might be where you have played team sports or activities.

TIP 8:

Top Tips

Practice a Mock Interview Before the Real Thing

During the selection process you will be required to sit a number of interviews, designed to test your suitability for joining the RAF. In addition to the assessable qualities that I have already provided, you will also be assessed on how well you present yourself during the interview.

The RAF recruitment officers are looking for your potential and ability to become a professional and competent member of their team. They are not looking for the finished article, but they certainly want to see potential. One of the most effective ways in which to prepare for the interview is to carry out a number of 'mock interviews' prior to the real thing. A mock interview is basically a practice run, where you'll get a friend or relative to ask you a series of questions, under formal conditions.

So, why is it important to carry out a mock interview? Well, look at it this way. Any team or professional individual will always practice their role before they do the real thing. An actor will rehearse his or her lines before filming, a football team will practice set pieces before a match and a professional swimmer will practice many lengths and improve their technique before their big race. Therefore, any serious candidate applying for a job should practice the interview beforehand. Not only will this allow them to increase their confidence, but it will go a long way to reducing nerves and fear.

During the real RAF interview, you need to create the right impression. The assessors will judge everything, from the clothes you wear to the way that you sit in the interview chair, so be prepared!

The interview is obviously an integral part of the selection process, and within this guide I have provided a section dedicated solely to this. Look at the sample interview questions and prepare your responses beforehand by way of a mock interview. Don't go into your interview unprepared. Instead, understand what is involved and what you need to do to impress the panel.

TIP 9:

Keep up-to-date with Current Affairs

In the build up to your selection interview, I would recommend that you keep up-to-date with current affairs, especially in relation to where the RAF are operating at the time of your application.

Try to watch the news and read newspaper articles, searching for information relating to any recent Armed Forces issues. These don't have to be specific to the Royal Air Force, but if you are joining a military organisation, then it would be wise for you to keep up to speed with current affairs. The type of newspaper that you read is important. Make sure you choose a quality newspaper that will provide you with accurate and up-to-date information.

During the interview, you may get asked a question along the following lines: 'Can you tell me whereabouts the RAF are operating in the world right now?' The only way to answer this question is by keeping up-to-date with current affairs and topical issues that are relevant to the RAF. I would also advise that you pick a few topical current affairs subjects, be aware of them, and also have an opinion of them. This will demonstrate to the recruitment staff, that you are fully aware of current topical issues and that you can also form an opinion of them.

The following websites are useful tools for researching information that is relevant to the UK Armed Forces and the Royal Air Force:

- www.raf.mod.uk
- www.mod.uk
- www.rafnews.co.uk
- www.rafcom.co.uk

Please note: How2Become LTD is not responsible for the content of any external websites.

TIP 10:

Get Some Experience of Being Self-Reliant

During the selection process, the RAF recruitment staff will want to see some experience of where you have either been self-reliant, or have been without home comforts for a period of time. The reason for this is simple; when you join the RAF you will embark on a nine week training course that will change your life forever. Not only will you be required to live with lots of other people in the same room, but you will also be required to fend for yourself.

Those people who have no experience of being self-reliant, or have never experienced 'communal living' will struggle with this new way of life. Of course, it's easy for anybody to say 'I won't have any problems with leaving home or with being self-reliant', but providing examples of where you have already done this is a different matter. Provide the interviewer or recruitment staff with examples of where you have been away from home for long periods such as camps, school trips or adventure trips. Tell them what activities you were involved in, and also any responsibilities you had whilst being away from home. If you have little or no experience so far of being self-reliant, then I recommend that you get some. There are plenty of opportunities available to you, such as going camping with friends for the weekend, or you could even go away on an adventure trip or a holiday. Whatever activity you decide to take part in, make sure it is safe.

BONUS TIP:

Learn the Values of the RAF

Any organisation or service worth its salt will develop a set of values or standards that it expects its employees to abide by. The reason why an organisation will develop these standards is because it wants to deliver or provide a very high level of service.

During your research into the RAF, I strongly recommend that you learn its values. When the recruitment officer at the Armed Forces Careers Office asks you 'what you have you learnt about the RAF', you will be able to tell him or her that you have taken the time to learn these important values, and also what they mean. These values are also known as 'core competencies'. As we explained earlier in the guide, the competencies include:

• Having self-respect, and being respectful of others;

• Having integrity, which means being responsible, honest and courageous;

• Having physical courage, loyalty, commitment and being able to work as part of a team during your service;

• Having personal excellence, being proud and self-disciplined;

The most effective way to memorise these values, is to simply remember the word 'RISE':

R = Respect

I = Integrity

S = Service

E = Excellence

In addition to a set of values, the RAF also has what is called an 'ethos' statement. This is basically a statement of how it intends to go about its business. The following is the RAF's ethos statement:

'Our distinctive character, spirit and attitude that is necessary to pull together as a team, in order to deliver air power no matter the challenges or environment. We place unit and Royal Air Force success above self and strive to be courageous in the face of adversity and risk. Sustained by strong leadership, high professional and personal standards, we are bound by a strong sense of tradition and belonging to an organization of which we are immensely proud' (Crown Copyright ©).

Make sure you learn the ethos statement and the values of the RAF before you go to your interview.

CHAPTER 3

*How To
Create A CV*

The first stage of the RAF selection process is to submit your application. However, before you get to this stage it is important to speak to an Armed Forces Careers advisor about the options that are available to you, and also about life as an RAF Reserve. You can find details of your nearest Armed Forces Careers Office by visiting the Royal Air Force website www.raf.mod.uk.

On the website you will also find plenty of information about life in the RAF and the careers that are available. You should also discuss your choice of career with your family and with your partner to ensure that you have their full support. When visiting the careers office, it is advisable that you take along an accurate and up-to-date CV.

During this chapter of the book, I will provide you with a step-by-step guide on how to create the ultimate CV!

The phrase Curriculum Vitae, translated, mean 'the course of life'. CVs are used to demonstrate to an employer that you have the potential, skills and experience to carry out the role you are applying for. Your CV is a very important document, and therefore you should spend a sufficient amount of time designing it so that it matches the job you are applying for.

WHAT MAKES AN EFFECTIVE CV?

In simple terms, an effective CV is one that matches the specification and the requirements of the job that you are applying for. Your CV should be used as a tool to assist you during the initial stages of the RAF selection process, and should be centred on the following areas:

• Creating the right impression of yourself;

• Indicating that you possess the right qualities and attributes to perform the role you are applying for;

- Grabbing the assessor's attention;

- Being clear and concise.

The most effective CV's are the ones that make the assessor's job easy. They are simple to read, to the point, relevant and focus on the job/role. CV's should not be overly long, unless an employer specifically asks for this. Effective CV writing is an acquired skill that can be obtained relatively quickly, with just a little bit of time, effort and focus.

Let's take a look at some of the skills and qualifications required to become a Physical Training Instructor in the RAF Reserve

Qualifications Required	About The Job
You will need 2 GCSEs/ or equivalent, in the subjects of English language at Grade C/3 minimum and in Mathematics at Grade G/6 minimum. You will need to have a good standard of fitness in a number of sports and have the ability to swim. You will be assessed via a specialist interview and be required to undertake additional tests.	Physical Training Instructors are responsible for organising and arranging physical fitness training programmes for all members of the RAF. Therefore a good standard of physical fitness and organisational skills are required. In addition to being physically fit you must also possess good motivational skills. • Manage and arrange adventure activities; • Manage sporting facilities; • Organise and conduct instructional classes; • Perform fitness tests; • Arrange and hold sports counselling sessions.

You will see from the above details that some of the key elements of the role include suitable levels of physical fitness, good organisational skills, motivational skills and the ability to manage people and resources. Once you have the above information, then you will be able to mould your CV around the key aspects of the job.

Before I provide you with a sample CV that is based on matching the above role, let's take a look at some of the key elements of a CV.

THE KEY ELEMENTS OF A CV

The following is a list of information that I recommend you include within your CV. Try to put them in this order, and remember to be brief and to the point. Make sure you include and highlight the positive aspects of your experience and achievements.

The layout of your CV should be as follows:

- **Your Personal Details;**
- **Your Profile;**
- **Your Employment History;**
- **Your Academic Achievements;**
- **Your Interests;**
- **Any 'Other' Information;**
- **Your References.**

Let's now take a look at each of the above sections and see what you need to include.

YOUR PERSONAL DETAILS

When completing this section, you should include the following details:

• Your Full Name;
• Address;
• Date of Birth;
• Nationality;
• Contact Telephone Numbers (home and mobile);
• E-mail Address.

YOUR PROFILE

To begin with, try to write a brief statement about yourself, making sure that you include keywords which best describe your character. Some effective words that you can use to describe yourself include: Ambitious, enthusiastic, motivated, caring, trustworthy, meticulous, sense of humour, drive, character, determination, will to succeed, passionate, loyal, teamwork and hard working.

The above words are all powerful and positive aspects of an individual's character. Think about your own character and what positive words could be used to describe you. Within your profile description, try to include a statement that is relative to you, which will persuade an assessor that you are the right person for the role:

"I am an extremely fit and active person who has a great deal of experience in this field and I have a track record of high achievement. I have exceedingly good organisational and motivational skills and I am always striving to improve myself. I believe that I would embrace the challenges that this new role has to offer".

YOUR EMPLOYMENT HISTORY

When completing this section, try to ensure that it is completed in reverse chronological order. Provide the reader with dates, locations and employers, and remember to include your job title. Give a brief description of your main achievements, and try to include words of a positive nature, such as: achieved, developed, progressed, managed, created, succeeded, devised, drove, expanded and directed.

It is also a good idea to quantify your main achievements, such as:

"During my time with this employer I was responsible for motivating my team and organising different activities".

YOUR ACADEMIC ACHIEVEMENTS

When completing this section, include the dates, names and locations of the schools, colleges or universities that you attended in chronological order. You should also include your qualifications and any other relevant achievements such as health and safety, or first aid qualifications. Anything that is relevant to the role that you are applying for would be an advantage.

YOUR INTERESTS

Within this section, try to include interests that match the requirements of the job, and ones that also portray you in a positive manner. Perhaps you have previously worked within the voluntary sector, or have even carried out some charity work in the past? If so, try to include these in your CV, as they show that you have a caring nature. You might also be someone who plays sports or keeps fit, in which case you should include this too. Any evidence of where you have worked effectively as part of a team will massively aid your application.

ANY 'OTHER' INFORMATION

Within this section of your CV, you can include any 'other' information that is relevant to your skills or experiences, that you may feel are of benefit. A good example of this is certificates of achievement, either from work, school or sporting activities.

REFERENCES

Although you will normally be required to provide two references as part of your application for joining the RAF, it is good practice to include these at the end of your CV. Try to include your current or previous employer, providing you know that they are going to write positive things about you. Be careful who you choose as a reference, and make sure that you seek their permission prior to putting down their name and contact details. It might also be a good idea to ask them if you can have a copy of what they have written about you for reference later.

SAMPLE CV

The following sample CV has been designed to give you an idea of how an effective CV might look. It has been created with the position of 'Physical Training Instructor' in mind. *Please note: All of the information provided is fictitious.*

Curriculum Vitae of Richard McMunn:

Address: 75, Any Street, Anytown, Anyshire, ANY 123.

DOB: 01/01/1970

Nationality: British

Telephone contact: 01227 123456 / Mobile 07890 123456

Email contact: RichardMcMunn@anyemailaddress.co.uk

Personal Profile of Richard McMunn:

I am an extremely fit and active person, who has a great deal of experience in this field. Furthermore, I have a track record of high achievement. I have very good organisational and motivational skills, and I am always striving to improve myself. I believe that I would embrace the challenges that this new role has to offer. I am a motivated, dedicated, loyal and ambitious person, who has the ability to work both as a team member and independently.

I already have a large amount of experience in the working environment, and take on a large number of responsibilities at work, at home and in my leisure time. I am currently the Captain of my local football team, and a part of my responsibilities include organising and conducting weekly evening training sessions for the team. For every training session that I run, I always try to vary the type of exercises that we perform. This allows me to maintain everyone's motivation and interest levels. For example, one week I will organise the Multi-Stage Fitness Test, and another week we will practice tackling and dribbling skills.

Employment History of Richard McMunn (in chronological order)**:**

Company/Organisation/Employer:

Position within company:

Dates of employment:

Summary of duties:

Academic Achievements of Richard McMunn:

Health and Safety Qualification
Date of achievement:

First Aid Qualification
Date of achievement:

Level 1 Physical Training Instructor Qualification
Date of achievement:

GCSE Maths Grade C
Date of achievement:

GCSE English Grade C
Date of achievement:

GCSE Physical Education Grade B
Date of achievement:

Interests and Hobbies of Richard McMunn

I am an extremely fit and active person, who carries out a structured training programme at my local gym five times a week. During my training sessions, I will carry out a variety of different exercises, including indoor rowing, cycling, treadmill work and light weights. I measure my fitness levels by performing the multi-stage fitness test once a week, and I can currently achieve level 14.5. In addition to my gym work I am a keen swimmer, and break up my gym sessions with long swim sessions twice a week. I can swim 60 lengths of my local swimming pool in a time of 35 minutes. I am also the Captain of my local football team, and am responsible for organising the weekly training sessions. In addition to my sporting activities, I like to relax with a weekly Yoga group at my local community centre. I also have a keen interest in art and attend evening classes from October through to December.

Further Information

Six months ago I decided to carry out a sponsored fitness event, in order to raise money for a local charity. I swam 60 lengths of my local swimming pool, and then ran 26 miles before cycling 110 miles all in one day. In total, I managed to raise over £10,000 for charity.

References

Name, address and contact details of reference #1

Name, address and contact details of reference #2

TOP TIPS FOR CREATING AN EFFECTIVE CV

Top Tips

New Application = New CV

It is important that every time you apply for a job, you revaluate the content of your CV, so that you can match the skills and qualifications required. As a rule, you should complete a new CV for every job application (unless the job you are applying for is very similar). Don't become complacent and allow your CV to get out of date.

Don't pad out your CV

There is a common misconception amongst many job applicants, that you need to make your CV several pages long in order for it to get recognised. This simply isn't true. When creating your CV, you should ALWAYS aim for quality over quantity. If I was looking through an applicant's CV, I would much prefer to see 3 pages of high quality focused information rather than 30 pages padded out with irrelevance.

Create a positive image

Writing an effective CV involves a number of important aspects. One of those is the manner in which you present it. When developing your CV, ask yourself the following questions:

- Is the spelling, grammar and punctuation correct?

- Is it legible and easy to read?

- Is the style in which you are writing your CV standardised?

- Is it neat?

- Is it constructed in a logical manner?

By following the above bullet points in respect of your CV, you will be on the right track to improving your chances of getting the job you are after. You should spend just as much time on the presentation of your CV as you do on the content.

Qualities and Attributes

When you are developing your CV, have a look at the required personal qualities that are listed within the job/person specification. Try to match these as closely as possible, but again, ensure that you provide examples where appropriate. For example, in the sample job description for a Physical Training Instructor, one of the required personal qualities was to 'organise and conduct instructional classes.' Try and provide an example of where you have achieved this in any previous roles. The following is a fictitious example of how this could be illustrated:

'I am currently the Captain of my local football team, and part of my responsibilities include conducting weekly evening training sessions for the team. For every training session that I run, I always try to vary the type of exercises that we perform. This allows me to maintain everyone's motivation and interest levels. For example, one week I will organise the Multi-Stage Fitness Test for them, and another week I will arrange practice tackling and dribbling skills'.

Remember that matching your qualities and attributes to the role you are applying for is essential!

Be honest when creating your CV

If you lie on your CV, especially when it comes to academic qualifications or experience, you will almost certainly get caught out at some point in the future. Maybe not straight away, but even a few months or years down the line, an employer can still dismiss you for incorrect information that you provided during the selection process. It simply isn't worth it. Be honest when creating your CV, and if you don't have the right skills for the job you are applying for, go out there and get them!

Now that I've shown you how to create an effective CV, schedule into your action plan a date and time for when you intend to create your own.

CHAPTER 4

*Online Application
Form*

Once you have decided that a career in the RAF is for you, then it is time to make your application. Remember, you are under no obligation to join the force until you sign your contract. There are two ways to apply. The first and most efficient method is to apply online via the website www.raf.mod.uk. The second is to complete the application form at your Armed Forces Careers Office. You will need to register your details with the RAF before commencing with your online application, which usually takes around 45 minutes to complete.

Below we have laid out an example of what the online application form will look like, along with detailed advice on how to answer some of the key sections.

SAMPLE RAF RESERVES ONLINE APPLICATION FORM

About You-

Name:

Surname:

Gender:

DOB:

Nationality:

Second Nationality (if applicable):

Address:

Home Phone Number:

Contact Phone Number:

Mobile Phone Number:

Religion:

UK National Insurance Number:

Birth Certificate Number:

Passport Number:

Passport Expiry Date:

Ethnic Background:

National Identity:

Do you have unrestricted right of residency in the UK or Ireland?
Yes/No

If no, please enter the following information about your Entry Stamp or your Visa-
Issue Date:
Expiry Date:

Ignoring periods spent aboard of 28 days or less, have you been a resident of the United Kingdom or Ireland for the last 5 years?
Yes/No

If no, please enter all countries of residence for the past 5 years, including dates.
Country:
Date Arrived/Date Left:

More About You-

Marital Status:

Does anyone depend on you for help and/or daily care?
Yes/No.

If yes, please provide additional details:

Nationality of Parents:
Father-
Mother-

Next of kin/who should be contacted in the event of an emergency?

Have you previously been under a care order?

Are you currently or have you recently been under a care order?
If yes, please provide details

Do you have a current account with a UK bank or building society?

Do you have any debts which you may struggle to pay back if you join the service?

Physical Fitness-

Please provide details of any sporting activities that you take part in:

Name of Sport:

Level or Qualification:

Hours spent per week:

Please provide details of any adventurous activities that you have taken part in, or regularly take part in:

Activity:

Level or Qualification:

Date participated:

Are you able to swim?
Yes/No

Please provide details of any other sporting/physically based hobbies and interests that you have:

Please provide details of any sporting/physically based responsibilities that you have held, for example team captain:

Please provide details of any uniformed organisations that you have been involved in as a member:

Do you have any debts which you may struggle to pay back if you join the service?

Have you ever been made bankrupt?

Medical-

Height (cm):

Weight (kg):

Do you wear glasses:

Do you wear contact lenses:

UK National Health Service Number:

Please provide the contact details for your Doctor/GP:

Drugs, Piercings and Tattoos-

Do you have any tattoos?

Do you have an understanding of the Armed Forces policy regarding tattoos?

Do you have any body piercings?

Do you have an understanding of the Armed Forces policy regarding body piercing?

Do you have an understanding of the Armed Forces policy regarding the misuse of drugs?

Driving License-

Are you in possession of a valid UK driving license?
Yes/No

Are you currently disqualified from driving?
Yes/No

If yes, what date are you disqualified until?

Finally, please provide details of any of your relatives that are currently serving in the Armed Forces, or who have been previously served in the Armed Forces (within the past 20 years). **Please do not include details of anyone who has or is currently serving in any special units, such as the SAS or SRR.**

Armed Forces Experience-

Are you currently serving in any British or Foreign Forces Regular or Reserve Armed Forces, including voluntary service as an Adult Cadet Instructor?

Have you previously served in any British or Foreign Forces Regular or Reserve Armed Forces, including voluntary service as an Adult Cadet Instructor?

Have you previously applied to join the Royal Air Force?
Yes/No

If yes, please provide details of your previous applications-

Have you previously applied to join the Royal Navy?
Yes/No

If yes, please provide details of your previous applications-

Have you previously applied to join the Army?
Yes/No

If yes, please provide details of your previous applications-

Education and Employment-

Which of the following best describes your current status:

[ ] Employed full-time.

[ ] Employed in a temporary position.

[ ] Work experience placement.

[ ] Performing voluntary work.

[ ] Apprentice.

[ ] Unemployed.

[ ] Still at secondary school.

[ ] In sixth form/college.

[ ] At university.

[ ] Gap year.

[ ] Part-time study.

[ ] Other.

Education Details-

In chronological (ascending) order, please list all schools, colleges and universities that you have attended from the age of 14 upwards:

Grades and Qualifications-

In chronological (ascending) order, please list all GCSE, A-Level, Diplomas, Certificates, Degrees or other qualifications that you have achieved, from the age of 14 upwards. This should include all forthcoming or predicted grades for the future, along with the date at which you expect to receive them.

Languages-

Using the boxes provided, please indicate whether you are fluent in any languages other than English, and to what extent.

Language 1:

Fluency:

Can you write in this language?

Can you read in this language?

Employment and Work Experience-

In this section, please provide details of up to 3 job roles or work experience placements (if relevant). You should enter these in chronological order (ascending).

Employer/Organisation:

Dates working in this position (From-To):

Position and Key Responsibilities:

Nature of role: **Full time/Part time/Temporary/Work Experience/Voluntary**

References-

In this section, please provide contact details for a minimum of 1 reference(s). Please be aware that we may contact this person when assessing your application form:

Entry Options-

In order of preference, please list which career group you would like to join in the RAF Reserves:

First Choice:

Second Choice:

Third Choice:

University Air Squadron: UAS Applicants Only-

If you want to join the UAS, tick the box below and select the appropriate unit:

[ ] I am applying to join the UAS

UAS Unit:

By this point, you will have reached the end of the application. You'll see two final questions. The first of these will invite you, very briefly, to explain what has prompted your interest in joining the RAF Reserves. This is fairly self-explanatory. Then, finally, you will be given a box that provides you with the opportunity to fill in 'additional information'. You should use this box as a chance to further explain your motivation for joining the Reserves. My advice is to think of this box as a question in itself.

Imagine that the question reads, 'Please tell us why you have decided to apply for the RAF Reserves'. How would you answer? Remember that this is your only real chance to impress the reader, so make it count! Your answer doesn't have to be long or extremely detailed, just as long as you properly convey your reasons for applying. If you can show a prior knowledge of the role itself, then even better. Do your research beforehand and then incorporate this into your response.

'Please tell us why you have decided to apply for the RAF Reserves'.

Sample Response:

'I have always been interested in joining the RAF, and I believe that a career as an RAF Reserve suits me perfectly. I am a committed, enthusiastic person who is passionate about protecting and safeguarding the British public. I believe that a career in the Reserves would suit me better than a career as a full time member of the service, as I have personal commitments that I will need to balance at the same time. However, I am fully prepared to drop these commitments if necessary, should the RAF require me to go into action. I am someone who believes strongly in honour, discipline, teamwork and integrity, and I know that all of these values are promoted and shared within the RAF. The reason that I have selected the role of Intelligence Analyst as my first choice is because I believe I would be extremely well suited to the position. I know that RAF Intelligence Analysts are responsible for supplying essential intelligence information to forces deployed around the world. I'm someone with fantastic analytical and decision making skills, who is highly proficient in IT based technology. Therefore, I believe that all of these competencies would make me a good fit for the role, and that working as a Reserve presents the ideal environment for me to learn and grow.

I would make a dedicated, passionate and skilled addition to the RAF Reserve team, and I would be extremely grateful if you would consider my application'.

Kind regards,

Once you have filled in the final section, check your application over thoroughly. Don't just read it yourself, give it to your friends and family to iron out any possible spelling errors or general mistakes. Remember that the RAF get many thousands of these applications, you need to do your best to stand out from the majority, who won't have checked their application over properly and won't have prepared by using the core competencies.

CHAPTER 5

Aptitude Tests

Once you have submitted your application form, you will face a short wait. Following this, if your application has been successful, you will be invited to attend a Squadron Information Day. Depending on the squadron that you are applying to, this day will take 1 of 2 potential forms:

- An open day, designed to further educate candidates on the role that they are applying for, providing them with the opportunity to ask questions and meet with other potential recruits.

- An open day, designed to further educate candidates on the role that they are applying for, providing them with the opportunity to ask questions and meet with other potential recruits, followed by a series of psychometric aptitude examinations.

When you receive your invitation to attend the information day, you will be informed on whether you will be required to take the aptitude tests on the day, or afterwards. Either way, you need to start preparing immediately. I cannot emphasise how important this is.

The tests that you will be required to take are extremely difficult and challenging, and the large majority of candidates will not be successful. The reason that these candidates will fail is because they lack preparation, and as a result will not have enough practice before the examination. Many candidates will wait until they receive their invite to the information day to start their preparation. This is a huge mistake. Once you've sent off your application form, start preparing immediately. If you can, you should even start preparing BEFORE sending off the application form.

To be successful in these assessments you will need to be as familiar as you possibly can with the type of questions you'll be answering. In this chapter, I'll show you how you can do this.

The aptitude tests that you will take are as follows:

- A **Verbal Reasoning Test:** assesses how well you can interpret written information. During this test you will have 15 minutes to answer 20 questions.

- A **Numerical Reasoning Test:** determines how accurately you can interpret numerical information such as charts, graphs and tables. The test will also assess your ability to use fractions, decimals and different formulae. There are two parts to this test. During the first test, you will have just 4 minutes to answer 12 questions that are based on fractions, decimals and formulae. During the second test, you will have 11 minutes to answer 15 questions that relate to different graphs and tables.

- A **Work Rate Test:** assesses how quickly and accurately you can carry out routine tasks. During this test you will have 4 minutes to answer 20 questions.

- A **Spatial Reasoning Test:** examines your ability to work with different shapes and objects. During this test you will have just 4 minutes to answer 10 questions.

- A **Mechanical Comprehension Test:** assesses how effectively you can work with different mechanical concepts. During this particular test, you will have 10 minutes in which to answer 20 questions.

- An **Electrical Comprehension Test:** assesses your ability to work with different electrical concepts. During this test you will have 11 minutes to complete 21 questions.

- A **Memory Test:** determines how accurately you can remember and recall information. There are two parts to this test, and you will have a total of 10 minutes in which to answer 20 questions.

Within this section of the guide, I will provide you with a number of hints, tips and practice questions to help you prepare for the real aptitude tests.

Please note that the questions provided are not the exact questions you'll encounter on the test day. The times that I have provided for each test are also different to the real aptitude tests.

Below are some useful tips to help further aid your preparation and improve your testing questions.

Top Tips

• Consider purchasing a 'psychometric test' booklet. This will give you further practice with sample test questions and will increase your knowledge and ability on each specific testing area. You can buy these from www.how2become.co.uk where there is also an 'Armed Forces Tests' guide available.

• Drink plenty of water in the days leading up to the test. This will ensure that your concentration levels are at their best. If you are dehydrated, then you are less likely to perform at your peak.

• Make sure that you get a good night's sleep before the actual test. You will find that your performance is much better when you are alert.

• Practice without a calculator. You may not be able to use one on the actual test day, so practising without one will prepare you beforehand.

• The tests usually take place at the RAF Careers Office. Make sure you get to the venue with plenty of time to spare. You are better off arriving 30 minutes early than 5 minutes late. Being late for the test will only make you more nervous.

- You do not need to take any writing implements with you on the day. The RAF Careers Office will provide you with any pens, paper or other stationery equipment required.

Now let's take a look at each of the different testing areas.

VERBAL REASONING TEST

During the aptitude tests, you will be required to sit a verbal reasoning assessment. This test will assess how well you can interpret written information.

On the following pages, you will find a number of practice verbal reasoning tests to assist you during your preparation. If, during the real test you find yourself struggling with a question, simply move onto the next one. However, remember to leave the answer sheet blank for the question that you haven't answered. If you have time at the end, you can go back to the questions you have left and have another go. If you are still unable to answer the question, then it is always worth 'guessing' as you still have a '1 in 5' chance of getting it right. In the real test, you won't have much time to complete the questions, so you must work quickly and accurately. Take a look at the exercises on the following pages. Allow yourself 30 minutes to answer the 21 questions. Write your answers down in the box provided.

Verbal Reasoning Sample Exercise

VERBAL REASONING

EXAMPLE 1

Read the following information carefully and answer the following question.

Car A is black in colour and has 4 months left on the current MOT. The tax is due in 8 months' time. The car has no service history and has completed 46,500 miles. The car has had 2 owners.

Car B is red in colour and has a full 12 months MOT. The tax is not due for another 8 months. The car has completed 14,459 miles and has only had 1 owner. There is a full service history with the car.

Car C has no tax. The MOT is due to run out in 3 months' time and the car has no service history. The speedometer reading is 121,000 miles and the car, which is black in colour, has had a total of 8 owners.

Car D is black in colour and has 7 months left on the current MOT. The tax is due in 8 months' time. The car has no service history and has completed 43,000 miles. The car has had 2 owners.

Car E has 5 months tax. The MOT runs out in 7 months' time. The car, which is red in colour, has a partial service history and has completed 87,000 miles. It has had a total of 3 owners.

Question
You want a car that is red in colour and has a full service history with less than 100,000 miles. Which car would you choose?

How to work it out

- Make sure you read the passage carefully. Pick out the key details from the question and determine which car is most suitable;

- You can automatically rule out Car A, C and D because they are not red in colour;

- You can rule out Car E because it only has a partial service history, therefore the correct answer is Car B.

Answer:
Car B

Now that you've seen a sample question, have a go at a real practice Verbal Reasoning Test.

You have 30 minutes in which to complete the 21 questions. Please note that the time limit placed on this exercise will not be the same as the one set during the real RAF Selection Test.

FLAT A is located in a town. It is 12 miles from the nearest train station. It has 2 bedrooms and is located on the ground floor. The monthly rental is £450 and the council tax is £50 per month. The lease is for 6 months.

FLAT B is located in the city centre and is 2 miles from the nearest train station. It is located on the 3rd floor. The monthly rental is £600 and the council tax is £130 per month. The lease is for 6 months and it has 3 bedrooms.

FLAT C is located in the city centre and is 3 miles from the nearest train station. It is located on the 1st floor and has 1 bedroom. The monthly rental is £550 and the council tax is £100 per month. The lease is for 12 months.

FLAT D is located in a village. The monthly rental is £395 per month and the council tax is £100 per month. It is located on the ground floor and the lease is for 12 months. It is 18 miles from the nearest train station. The flat has 2 bedrooms.

FLAT E is located in a village and is 12 miles from the nearest train station. It has 3 bedrooms and is located on the 2nd floor. The monthly rental is £375 and the council tax is £62. The lease is for 12 months.

Question 1

You want a flat that is within 10 miles of the nearest train station and is located on the 1st floor or lower. The combined monthly rent/council tax bill must be no greater than £600.

A – Flat A

B – Flat B

C – Flat C

D – Flat D

E – None

Answer

Question 2

You want a flat that has at least 2 bedrooms and has a combined monthly rent/council tax bill which does not exceed £450.

A – Flat A

B – Flat B

C – Flat C

D – Flat D

E – Flat E

Answer

Question 3

You want a flat that has a combined monthly rent/council tax bill that is not in excess of £600, is within 20 miles of the nearest train station, and has a lease of 6 months.

A – Flat A

B – Flat B

C – Flats A or D

D – Flats A or E

E – Flats C or D

Answer [   ]

Barry and Bill work at their local supermarket in the town of Whiteman. Barry works every day except Wednesdays. The supermarket is run by Barry's brother Elliott, who is married to Sarah.

Sarah and Elliott have 2 children called Marcus and Michelle, who are both 7 years old. They live in a road adjacent to the supermarket.

Barry lives in a town called Redford which is 7 miles from Whiteman. Bill's girlfriend Maria, works in a factory in her hometown of Brownhaven. The town of Redford is 4 miles from Whiteman and 6 miles from the seaside town of Tenford.

Sarah and Elliott take their children on holiday to Tenford twice a year and Barry usually gives them a lift in his car. Barry's mum lives in Tenford and he tries to visit her once a week at 2pm, on a day he is not working.

Question 4

Which town does Elliot live in?

A – Redford

B – Whiteman

C – Brownhaven

D – Tenford

E – Cannot say

Answer

Question 5

On which day of the week does Barry visit his mother?

A – Monday

B – Tuesday

C – Wednesday

D – Friday

E – Whenever he can.

Answer

Question 6

Bill and Maria live together in Brownhaven?

A – True

B – False

C – Impossible to say

Answer

Janet and Steve have been married for 27 years. They have a daughter called Jessica who is 25 years old. They all want to go on holiday together but cannot make up their minds where to go.

Janet's first choice would be somewhere hot and sunny abroad. Her second choice would be somewhere in their home country that involves a sporting activity. She does not like hill-climbing or walking holidays, but her third choice would be a skiing holiday.

Steve's first choice would be a walking holiday in the hills somewhere in their home country and his second choice would be a sunny holiday abroad. He does not enjoy skiing.

Jessica's first choice would be a skiing holiday and her second choice would be a sunny holiday abroad. Jessica's third choice would be a walking holiday in the hills of their home country.

Question 7

Which holiday are all the family most likely to go on together?

A – Skiing

B – Walking

C – Sunny holiday abroad

D – Sporting activity holiday

E – None

Answer

Question 8

If Steve and Jessica were to go on holiday together, where would they be most likely to go?

A – Sunny holiday abroad

B – Skiing

C – Sporting activity holiday

D – Walking

E – Other

Answer

Question 9

Which holiday are Janet and Steve most likely to go on together?

A – Sunny holiday abroad

B – Skiing

C – Sporting activity holiday

D – Walking

E – Other

Answer

You're twice as likely to die in a fire at home if you do not have a working smoke alarm. A smoke alarm is the most effective way of alerting you and your family to the dangers of a fire. This will give you precious time to escape and get out safely. They are relatively cheap, easy to get hold of and simple to fit. However, many people who have smoke alarms are in danger too. The alarm could be in the wrong place, there may not be enough of them, or the battery could be missing/not working.

Question 10

You are less likely to die in a fire at home if you have a working smoke alarm.

A – True

B – False

C – Impossible to say

Answer

Question 11

Many people who have smoke alarms are still in danger.

A – True

B – False

C – Impossible to say

Answer

Question 12

If the smoke alarm does not conform to the relevant British Standards, there is still the possibility that it will not work effectively in the event of a fire.

A – True

B – False

C – Impossible to say

Answer

Approximately two thirds of all domestic fires are cooking-related. That's a lot of fires. The kitchen is the single most dangerous place in the home.

Time and time again, it's the same problems that cause fires in the kitchens up and down the UK. If you know what these problems are, the chances of having a fire in the kitchen are greatly reduced.

Question 13

The kitchen is one of the safest places in the home.

A – True

B – False

C – Impossible to say

Answer

Question 14

Overheated chip pans are the biggest cause of fires in the kitchen.

A – True

B – False

C – Impossible to say

Answer

Question 15

It is the same problems that cause fires in kitchens up and down the UK.

A – True

B – False

C – Impossible to say

Answer [ ]

Electricity is everywhere in our homes, and plays an important part in our lives. It only takes one badly wired plug to prove just how powerful electricity is. The wires don't even need to touch for a spark to jump and a fire to start. You should never become complacent where electricity is concerned. Just because there's no flame, doesn't mean there's no fire risk. The major rule where fires are concerned is that you should not put people's lives at risk. Get everyone out of your home and call the Fire Service.

Question 16

Complacency is a must where fire is concerned.

A – True

B – False

C – Impossible to say

Answer [ ]

Question 17

Where fire is concerned, people's safety is a must. You should get everyone out and call the Fire Service.

A – True

B – False

C – Impossible to say

Answer

Question 18

You should never put water on an electrical fire.

A – True

B – False

C – Impossible to say

Answer

A row of terraced houses was partially destroyed by an explosion on the 17th of April 2015. Just before the explosion, a man was seen running back into his house. He had reported a gas leak to the gas board 7 days prior to the explosion. The following facts are also known about the incident:

- The smell of gas had also been reported by two further residents in the weeks leading up to the explosion.

- The police are investigating possible terrorist connections with one of the residents.

Question 19

A gas leak was reported to the gas board on the 10th of April 2015.

A – True

B – False

C – Impossible to say

Answer

Question 20

The explosion was caused by a gas leak.

A – True

B – False

C – Impossible to say

Answer

Question 21

The man seen running back into his house had already reported a gas leak to the gas board.

A – True

B – False

C – Impossible to say

Answer

ANSWERS TO VERBAL REASONING

Q1. E = none

EXPLANATION = you want a flat within 10 miles of the train station – this rules out answers A and D. You want a flat that is located on the 1st floor or lower – this rules out answer B. You want the rent and council tax to be no greater than £600 – this rules out answer C. Therefore, the correct answer is 'none'.

Q2. E = flat E

EXPLANATION = you want a flat that has at least 2 bedrooms – this rules out answer C. You want a flat with a combined cost for tax and rent to exceed no more than £450 – this rules out answers A, B and D. Therefore the correct answer is 'flat E'.

Q3. A = flat A

EXPLANATION = you want a flat with a combined cost for tax and rent to exceed no more than £600 – this rules out flats B and C. You want a flat that has a lease for 6 months – this rules out flat D and E. So your remaining option is flat A.

Q4. B = Whiteman

EXPLANATION = Elliott lives in the town of Whiteman.

Q5. C = Wednesday

EXPLANATION = Barry tries to visit his mum on Wednesdays at 2pm. (It's the only day he has off from work).

Q6. C = impossible to say

EXPLANATION = you are not told whether Maria and Bill live together.

Q7. C = sunny holiday abroad

EXPLANATION = they are most likely to go on a sunny holiday abroad. They all mention a sunny holiday abroad as one of their choices.

Q8. A = sunny holiday abroad

EXPLANATION = Jessica and Steve are most likely to go on a sunny holiday abroad.

Q9. A = sunny holiday abroad

EXPLANATION = Steve and Janet are most likely to go on a sunny holiday abroad.

Q10. A = true

EXPLANATION = the passage clearly states that you are less likely to die if you have a working smoke alarm fitted in your home.

Q11. A = true

EXPLANATION = the passage clearly states that many people who do have a smoke alarm are still in danger too.

Q12. C = impossible to say

EXPLANATION = this statement is impossible to conclude from the passage. The passage does not mention anything in regards to British Standards, therefore you cannot make any assumptions based on the information provided.

Q13. B = false

EXPLANATION = this statement contradicts the passage. The passage highlights how the kitchen is one of the most dangerous places in the home.

Q14. C = impossible to say

EXPLANATION = the passage does not give any examples as to the causes of these kitchen fires, therefore you cannot assume this to be an example.

Q15. A = true

EXPLANATION = the statement reinforces how the same problems are occurring up and down the UK, so therefore this statement is true.

Q16. B = false

EXPLANATION = this contradicts the passage as it states 'you should never become complacent where electricity is concerned'. Therefore this statement would be false.

Q17. A = true

EXPLANATION = this statement reinforces what the passage is saying, and therefore is true.

Q18. C = impossible to say

EXPLANATION = whilst it is common sense that you shouldn't use water to put out an electrical fire, it is not actually stated in the passage, therefore you cannot assume this to be true.

Q19. A = true

EXPLANATION = a gas leak was reported to the gas board on the 10th April 2015, so therefore this statement is true.

Q20. C = impossible to say

EXPLANATION = the passage does not confirm that the explosion was caused by the gas leak, therefore it is impossible to say.

Q21. A = true

EXPLANATION = this statement reinforces the passage's claim that 'a man was seen running back into his house. He had reported a gas leak to the gas board 7 days prior to the explosion'. Therefore this statement must be true.

NUMERICAL REASONING TEST

During the aptitude tests, you will be required to sit a numerical reasoning assessment. This test is used to determine how accurately you can interpret numerical information such as charts, graphs and tables. The test will also assess your ability to use fractions, decimals and different formulae. As you can imagine, the most effective way to prepare for this type of test is to carry out lots of sample numerical reasoning test questions, without the aid of a calculator.

During the actual numerical reasoning test with the RAF, you will have a specific amount of time to answer each question. It is important that you do not spend too much time on one particular question.

Remember to check your answers very carefully. It is important that you check any incorrect answers to see why you got them wrong. Take a look at the sample exercise below, and then have a go at our sample Numerical Reasoning Test. You have 12 minutes in which to answer the 20 questions.

Calculators are not permitted.

Numerical Reasoning Sample Exercise

NUMERICAL REASONING

EXAMPLE 1

Add these fractions.

$$\frac{5}{7} + \frac{3}{5}$$

$$\frac{5}{7} \times \frac{3}{5} = \frac{25 + 21}{35} = \frac{46}{35} = 1\frac{11}{35}$$

Crossbow Method:

- The CROSS looks like a multiplication sign and it tells you which numbers to multiply together;

- One arm is saying 'multiply the 5 by the 5', and the other arm is saying 'multiply the 7 by the 3';

- The BOW says 'multiply the 2 numbers I am pointing at'. That is 7 times 5;

- The answer is 35 and it goes underneath the line in the answer.

EXAMPLE 2

Subtract these fractions.

$$\frac{4}{7} - \frac{2}{5}$$

$$\frac{4}{7} \times \frac{2}{5} = \frac{20 - 14}{35} = \frac{6}{35}$$

- To subtract fractions, the method is exactly the same. The only difference is, you minus the two numbers forming the top of the fraction, as opposed to adding them.

NUMERICAL REASONING

EXAMPLE 3

Multiply these fractions.

$$\frac{2}{3} \times \frac{4}{7}$$

$$\frac{2}{3} \times \frac{4}{7} = \frac{8}{21}$$

Arrow Method:

*   Multiplying fractions is easy. Draw an arrow through the two top numbers of the fraction, draw a line through the two bottom numbers (as shown above) and then multiply – simple!

*   Sometimes the fraction can be simplified, but in the above example, the answer is already in its simplest form.

EXAMPLE 4

Divide these fractions.

$$\frac{3}{7} \div \frac{1}{3}$$

$$\frac{3}{7} \times \frac{3}{1} = \frac{3}{7} \times \frac{3}{1} = \frac{9}{7} = 1\frac{2}{7}$$

*   Most people think that dividing fractions is difficult. It's not! It's actually relatively simple if you have mastered multiplying fractions.

*   Mathematicians realised that if you turned the second fraction upside down (as in the above example), and then change the 'divide' sum to a 'multiply', you will get the correct answer every time!

NUMERICAL REASONING

You have 12 minutes in which to complete the 20 questions. Please note that the time limit placed on this exercise will not be the same as the one set during the real RAF Selection Test.

Question 1

The two way table below compares pupils' results for GCSE English with GCSE Media grades.

English GCSE Grades	A*	A	B	C	D	E	F	U	Total
Media GCSE Grades									
A*									
A		2	2	3					7
B		1	3	4				1	9
C			8	10	6	1			25
D				1		2			3
E								1	1
F									
U									
Total		3	13	18	6	3		2	45

The percentage of pupils who received a D grade in Media is approximately what? To the nearest whole number.

Answer [   ]

Question 2

Which of the following is not a fraction equivalent to 4/7?

A – 40/70

B – 24/42

C – 12/21

D – 8/14

E – 1/4

Answer

Question 3

What is 36/50 in its simplest form?

A – 1/5

B – 1/8

C – 12/20

D –18/25

E – 5/10

Answer

Question 4

What is 789.21 + 3415.25?

Answer

Question 5

What is 14% of 3658?

Answer

Question 6

A travel company sells 3080 UK holidays in 2014. It is expected that the number of sales will increase by 14% each year. Work out the number of UK holidays the company expects to sell in 2015. Round all numbers up to the nearest whole number.

Answer

Question 7

In England, if the petrol consumption per day dropped by 8% from 2014 to 2015, how much would the petrol consumption be in 2015?

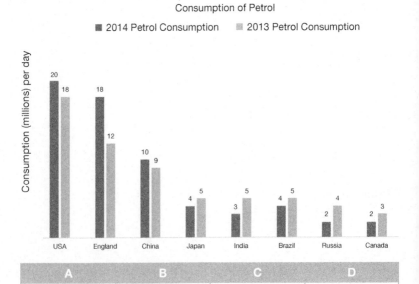

Consumption of Petrol

■ 2014 Petrol Consumption   ▨ 2013 Petrol Consumption

A	B	C	D
14,000,000	16,560,000	18,250,000	14,125,500

Question 8

Using the above chart, what is the percentage decrease for the USA between 2014 compared to that of the previous year?

A	B	C	D
15%	2%	1%	10%

Question 9

What is 40% of 360?

Answer | |

Question 10

What is 1/4 of 70?

Answer | |

Question 11

In the following question what is the value of t?

$$\frac{5\,(t - 32)}{2} = 5$$

Answer | |

Question 12

In the following question what is the value of t?

$$\frac{3(t + 35)}{6} = 35$$

Answer

Question 13

In the following question what is the value of t?

$$\frac{9(t + 16)}{5} = 144$$

Answer

Question 14

In the following question what is the value of t?

$$\frac{4(t - 16)}{32} = 2$$

Answer

Question 15

Convert 0.7 to a fraction

A – 7/10
B – 3/4
C – 75/1
D – 1/10
E – 2/3

Answer

Question 16

Convert 2.5 to a fraction

A – 25/10
B – 3/6
C - 2 1/2
D - 1/25
E - 2 2/1

Answer

Question 17

Convert 3.75 to a fraction

A – 75/1
B – 1/375
C – 3 1/75
D – 75/3
E – 3 3/4

Answer

Question 18

Convert 3/10 to a decimal

A – 3.0
B – 0.3
C – 3.33
D – 0.03
E – 0.003

Answer

Question 19

Convert 1/4 to a decimal

A – 0.025
B – 2.5
C – 0.25
D – 0.4
E – 4.0

Answer

Question 20

Convert 4/5 to a decimal

A – 0.08
B – 8.0
C – 4.5
D – 5.4
E – 0.8

Answer

ANSWERS TO NUMERICAL REASONING

Q1. 13%

EXPLANATION = number of pupils who received a D grade in Media = 6.

Total number of pupils = 45.

So, 6 ÷ 45 x 100 = 13.333%. To the nearest whole number = 13%.

Q2. E = 1/4

EXPLANATION = 1/4 is not equivalent to 4/7.

Q3. D = 18/25

EXPLANATION = 36/50 in its simplest form is 18/25 (both numbers can be divided by 2).

Q4. 4204.46

EXPLANATION = 789.21 + 3415.25 = 4204.46

Q5. 512.12

EXPLANATION = 14% of 3658 = 3658 ÷ 100 x 14 = 512.12

Q6. 3511

EXPLANATION = 3080 ÷ 100 x 114% (increase) = 3511.2. To the nearest whole number = 3511

Q7. B = 16,560,000

EXPLANATION = 18,000,000 ÷ 100 x 92(%) = 16,560,000

Q8. D = 10% decrease

EXPLANATION = the difference between 2014 and 2013 = 20,000,000 – 18,000,000 = 2,000,000. So 2,000,000 ÷ 20,000,000 x 100 = 10% decrease

Q9. 144

EXPLANATION = 360 ÷ 100 x 40 = 144

Q10. 17.5

EXPLANATION = 70 ÷ 4 = 17.5

Q11. 34

EXPLANATION = 5 x 34 – 32 ÷ 2 = 5

Q12. 35

EXPLANATION = 3 x 35 + 35 ÷ 6 = 35

Q13. 5

EXPLANATION = 9 x 5 x 16 ÷ 5 = 144

Q14. 20

EXPLANATION = 4 x 20 – 16 ÷ 32 = 2

Q15. A = 7/10

EXPLANATION = 0.7 x 100 = 70%. 70% = 70/100 = 7/10.

Q16. C = 2 ½

EXPLANATION = to convert 2.5 into a fraction = 25/10 = 5/2 = 2 ½

Q17. E = 3 ¾

EXPLANATION = to convert 3.75 into a fraction = 375/100 = 15/4 = 3 ¾

Q18. B = 0.3

EXPLANATION = to convert 3/10 into a decimal = 3 ÷ 10 = 0.3

Q19. C = 0.25

EXPLANATION = to convert ¼ into a decimal = 1 ÷ 4 = 0.25

Q20. E = 0.8

EXPLANATION = to convert 4/5 into a decimal = 4 ÷ 5 = 0.8

WORK RATE TEST

During the aptitude tests, you will be required to sit a work rate assessment. This form of test assesses your ability to work quickly and accurately whilst carrying out routine tasks. Before we move on to the test questions, let's take a look at a sample question.

Work Rate Sample Exercise

WORK RATE

EXAMPLE 1

Which of the answers below is an alternative code for **563**?

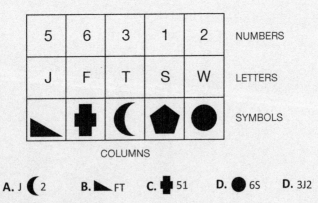

How to work it out

- You will be given a code consisting of numbers, letters or symbols. Your task is to look at the 5 provided alternatives, and decide which one uses the SAME columns as the original code;

WORK RATE

- As you can see in the above example, 563 uses the 1st column, the 2nd column and the 3rd column (in that order). So the code must use these columns in order in which they appear;

- You can see that answer B has the same code as 563. The triangle is taken from the 1st column, the 'F' is taken from the 2nd column and the 'T' is taken from the 3rd column.

Answer

B. ◣ FT

Things to remember:

- Make sure you pay careful attention to which columns are being used;

- I would suggest numbering the columns used (i.e. 1st, 2nd, 3rd), so when it comes to working out which answer is correct, you know which columns are being used.

WORK RATE TEST

You have 8 minutes in which to complete the 20 questions. Please note that the time limit placed on this exercise will not be the same as the one set during the real RAF Selection Test.

Question 1

Which of the below answers is an alternative to the code **G34**?

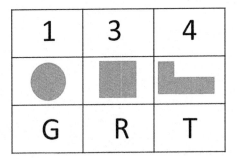

A. ▄▄R1   **B.** 14R   **C.** ●R T   **D.** TR ●

Answer

Question 2

Which of the below answers is an alternative to the code **CZF**?

Z	X	C
E	F	L
2	0	7

A. 72X   **B.** X02   **C.** LZE   **D.** F7L

Answer

Question 3

Which of the below answers is an alternative to the code **NS4**?

A. G7⬤   **B.** 4N7   **C.** ⬤✖7   **D.** G✖⬇

Answer

Question 4

Which of the below answers is an alternative to the code **1BM**?

★	★	☀	◆
3	1	A	K
M	P	0	B

A. ◆0A   **B.** PK★   **C.** P◆A   **D.** 30B

Answer [   ]

Question 5

Which of the below answers is an alternative to the code **DP6**?

A	H	3	6
2	D	B	C
P	8	Q	9

A. 298   **B.** Q69   **C.** H2B   **D.** 829

Answer [   ]

Question 6

Which of the below answers is an alternative to the code **BO3**?

H	➡	5	⬅
6	B	⬇	O
Y	1	3	⬆

A. 1⬆⬇   **B.** 1⬅Y   **C.** 61O   **D.** ➡51

Answer [   ]

Question 7

Which of the below answers is an alternative to the code **JX8**?

X	◣	J	1
C	5	◢	8
◺	H	◔	◿

A. ◣C1   **B.** 8◔5   9 **C.** ◔HC   **D.** ◥◔◣

Answer [   ]

Question 8

Which of the below answers is an alternative to the code **6SH**?

3	R	1	2	N	S
0	4	6	Y	Z	9
H	Q	V	C	M	7

A. 97Y   **B.** VZ3   **C.** 190   **D.** 3MC

Answer

Question 9

Which of the below answers is an alternative to the code **QEA**?

Q	9	5	A
1	B	E	4

A. 145   **B.** 1   **C.** B4   **D.** 41

Answer

Question 10

Which of the below answers is an alternative to the code **VFU**?

			8
F	5	U	V
	9		4
S		Z	

A. 5ZV   **B.** S9   **C.** 4S   **D.** 4S

Answer

Question 11

Which of the below answers is an alternative to the code **KCH**?

A	B	C	D
Q	R	S	T
K	J	I	H

A. JHK   **B.** AIR   **C.** QSD   **D.** IHJ

Answer

Question 12

Which of the below answers is an alternative to the code **GYL**?

Y	R	✖
U	⬤	B
✦	G	L

A. RUB   **B.** BLG   **C.** ⬤ UR   **D.** RL ✖

Answer

Question 13

Which of the below answers is an alternative to the code **931**?

2	6	9
7	3	5
1	0	4

A. 361   **B.** 164   **C.** 407   **D.** 560

Answer

Question 14

Which of the below answers is an alternative to the code **3MV**?

6	G	L
2	3	B
M	8	V

A. 82B   **B.** GB2   **C.** LG8   **D.** 28B

Answer

Question 15

Which of the below answers is an alternative to the code **H4EC**?

5	H			P	L
			4		
E	R			K	C

A. KEP   **B.** R5K   **C.**5L   **D.** PLCR

Answer

Question 16

Which of the below answers is an alternative to the code **E7B**?

X	4	7	J
W	3		F
E	P		B

A. WX   **B.** FBE   **C.** P3J   **D.** W F

Answer

Question 17

Which of the below answers is an alternative to the code **DU1**?

	E	Q	
	7	W	A
1	D		U

A. 7A   **B.** 1 W   **C.** AUW   **D.** DU

Answer

Question 18

Which of the below answers is an alternative to the code **HSP9**?

◗	F	W	8	3	H
R	✚	S	◖	P	⬍
9	▶	≠	I	✖	L

A. F ◖ ▲ ≠   **B.** ◖ IPL   **C.** LW3R   **D.** R ✚ ✚ L

Answer

Question 19

Which of the below answers is an alternative to the code **P5X**?

⬆	H	5	X
T	✚	8	N
P	✖	0	⬍
4	★	F	1

A. TON   **B.** ⬆ 8H   **C.** 1F ⬆   **D.** FTN

Answer

Question 20

Which of the below answers is an alternative to the code **NUA**?

●	S	J	7
U	✳	N	A
1	T	◕	✛

A. ATS   **B.** J17   **C.** 71U   **D.** ✳UN

Answer [   ]

ANSWERS TO WORK RATE TEST

Q1. C

Q2. A

Q3. D

Q4. B

Q5. D

Q6. A

Q7. A

Q8. C

Q9. B

Q10. D

Q11. C

Q12. A

Q13. C

Q14. A

Q15. C

Q16. D

Q17. A

Q18. C

Q19. A

Q20. B

SPATIAL REASONING TEST

During the aptitude tests, you will be required to sit a spatial reasoning assessment. The definition of spatial reasoning is as follows:

'The ability to interpret and make drawings from mental images and visualise movement or change in those images.'

During the test you will be confronted with a number of spatial reasoning questions. The only effective way to prepare for them is to practise as many as you can. You will find that the more questions you try, the quicker you will become at answering them. Although the examples I have provided in this section of the guide are timed, I would recommend that you take the time following the test to look at how the answers are reached. This is just as important as practising the tests under timed conditions.

Spatial Reasoning Sample Exercise

SPATIAL REASONING

EXAMPLE 1

Take a look at the following 3 shapes. Note the letter on the side of each shape.

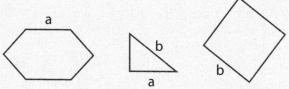

Join all of the 3 shapes together with the corresponding letters to make the following shape:

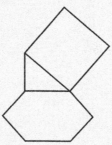

- Remember, for this type of question, you must use the letters to determine where each of the shapes will be positioned. The letters will refer to the side of a shape, which will then need to be connected to the side of another shape which also contains that letter.

Things to remember:

- The definition of spatial reasoning is as follows:

"The ability to interpret and make drawings from mental images and visualise movement or change in those images".

- Sketch out the individual shapes and then piece them together (like a jigsaw); this will allow you to visualise where each shape will be positioned;

- The more you practice these types of questions, the more competent you will become at working through them, and you will not have to rely on drawing the shapes out each time.

SPATIAL REASONING TEST

You have 8 minutes in which to complete the 20 questions. Please note that the time limit placed on this exercise will not be the same as the one set during the real RAF Selection Test.

For the following 20 questions, the question is as follows: connect the shapes using the corresponding letters to complete the shape.

Question 1

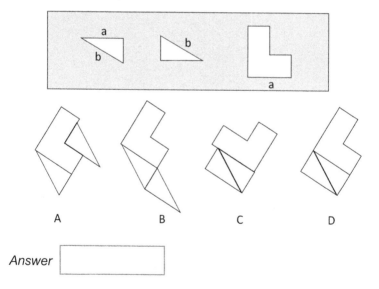

Answer

Question 2

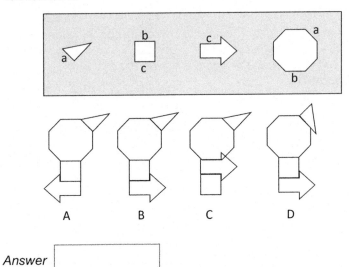

Answer [   ]

Question 3

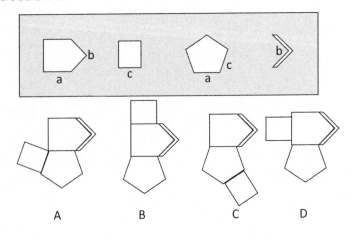

Answer [   ]

Question 4

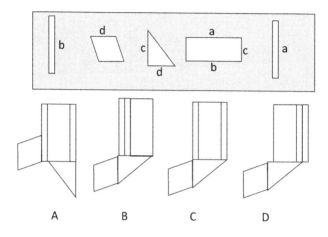

Answer

Question 5

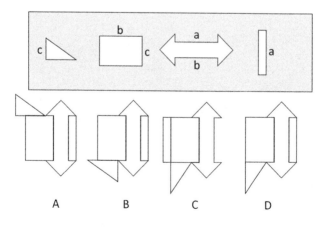

Answer

Question 6

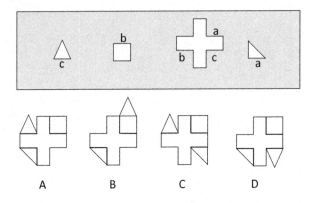

A   B   C   D

Answer

Question 7

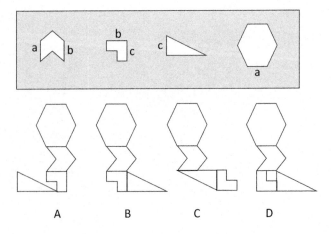

A   B   C   D

Answer

Question 8

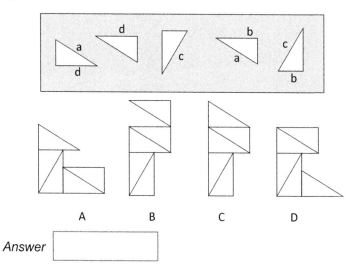

A   B   C   D

Answer

Question 9

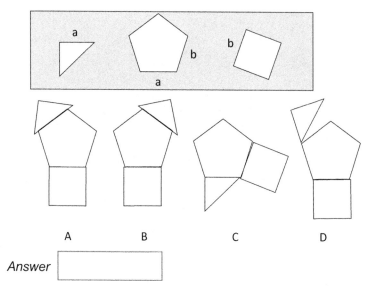

A   B   C   D

Answer

Question 10

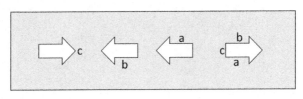

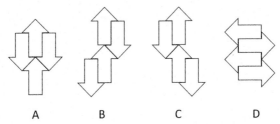

A   B   C   D

Answer

Question 11

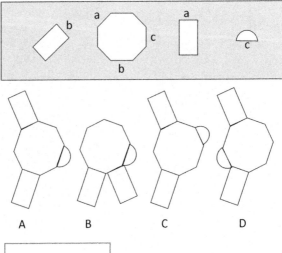

A   B   C   D

Answer

Question 12

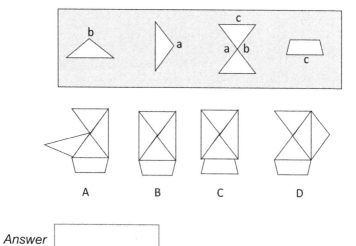

Answer

Question 13

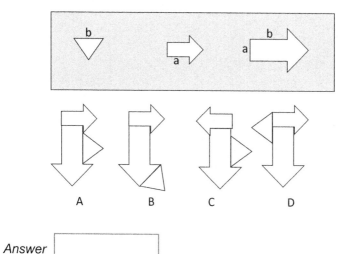

Answer

Question 14

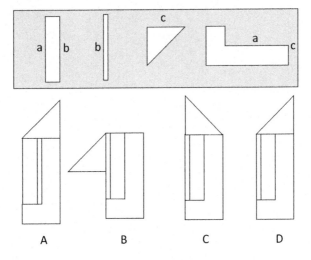

Answer

Question 15

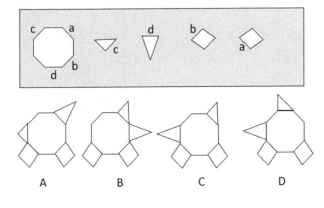

Answer

Question 16

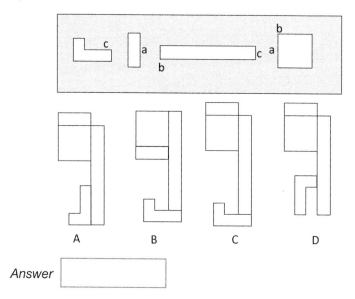

Answer

Question 17

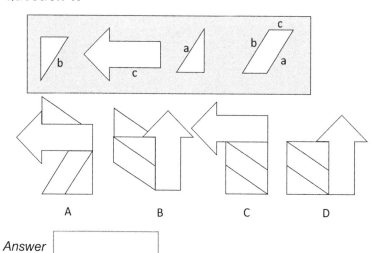

Answer

Question 18

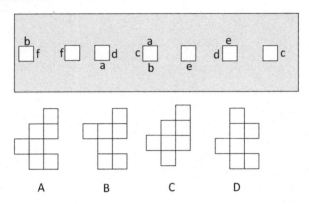

Answer

Question 19

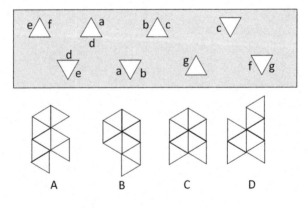

Answer

Question 20

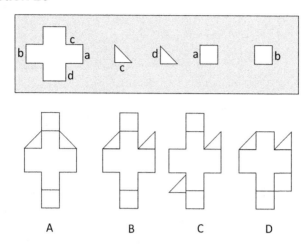

A   B   C   D

Answer

ANSWERS TO SPATIAL REASONING

Q1. D

Q2. B

Q3. A

Q4. C

Q5. D

Q6. A

Q7. B

Q8. C

Q9. C

Q10. A

Q11. A

Q12. B

Q13. A

Q14. D

Q15. C

Q16. C

Q17. D

Q18. A

Q19. C

Q20. B

MECHANICAL COMPREHENSION TEST

Mechanical Comprehension tests are an assessment that measures an individual's ability to understand mechanical concepts.

The majority of mechanical comprehension tests require a working knowledge of basic mechanical operations and the application of physical laws. On the following pages, I have provided you with a number of example questions to help you prepare for the tests. Work through them as quickly as possible but remember to go back through and check which ones you get wrong; and more importantly, make sure you understand how the correct answer is reached.

Mechanical Comprehension Sample Exercise

MECHANICAL COMPREHENSION

EXAMPLE 1

If the pulley is fixed, then the force required is equal to the weight. A simple way to work out how to calculate the force that is required, is to divide the weight by the number of sections of rope supporting it.

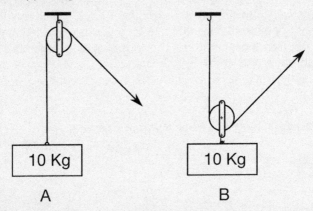

Diagram A = there is only one section of rope supporting the weight, therefore this can be worked out by = 10 ÷ 1 = 10.

Diagram B = there are two ropes supporting the weight, therefore this can be worked out by: 10 (weight) ÷ 2 (number of ropes supporting the weight) = 5.

MECHANICAL COMPREHENSION

EXAMPLE 2

When springs are arranged in a series, each spring can be the subject of the force applied. If the springs are arranged in a parallel line, the force is divided equally between them.

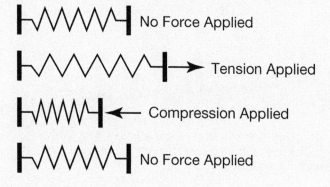

No Force Applied

Tension Applied

Compression Applied

No Force Applied

MECHANICAL COMPREHENSION

EXAMPLE 3

If the gears are connected by a chain or belt, then the gears will all move in the same direction.

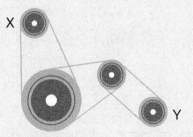

If the gears are touching, then adjacent gears move in the opposite direction. In the example below, X and Y will move in opposite directions.

MECHANICAL COMPREHENSION TEST

You have 12 minutes in which to complete the 20 questions. Please note that the time limit placed on this exercise will not be the same as the one set during the real RAF Selection Test.

Question 1

Which load weighs less?

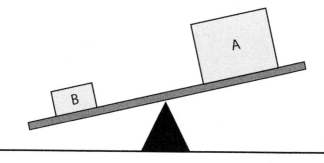

Answer

Question 2

At which point will the beam balance?

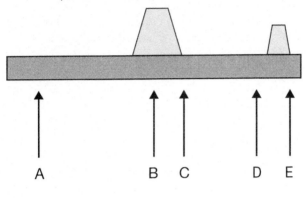

Answer

Question 3

Which post is carrying the greatest load?

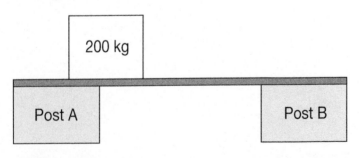

A	B	C
Post A	Post B	Both the same

Question 4

The following four containers are filled with clean water to the same level, which is 2 metres in height. If you measured the pressure at the bottom of each container once filled with water, which container would register the highest reading? If you think the reading would be the same for each container, then your answer should be E.

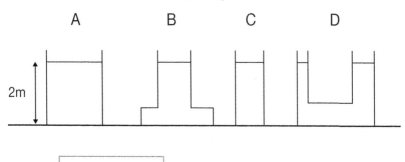

Answer

Question 5

If cog A turns anti-clockwise, which way will cog D turn?

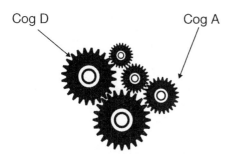

A	B	C
Clockwise	Anti-clockwise	Backwards and forwards

Question 6

Which weight requires the most force to lift it?

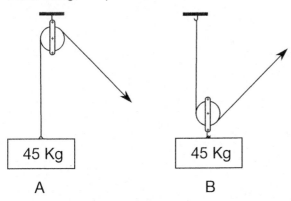

A	B	C
Both the same	A	B

Question 7

If wheel A is three times the diameter of wheel B and it rotates at 35rpm, what speed will wheel B rotate at?

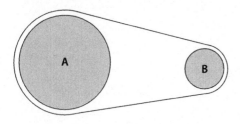

A	B	C
105 rpm	25 rpm	85 rpm

Question 8

On which pole is there the least pressure?

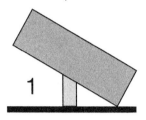 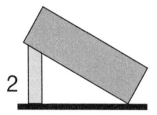

A	B
Pole 1	Pole 2

Question 9

If input effort is 750 ft.lb, what output effort will be produced by a machine with a mechanical advantage of 3?

Answer

Question 10

In the diagram, two wheels attached by a belt drive have the ratio of 3: 1. The smaller wheel has a 10cm circumference. How fast would the smaller wheel turn if the larger wheel turned at a rate of 450 rpm?

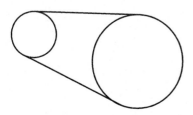

A	B	C	D
1300 rpm	1350 rpm	750 rpm	700 rpm

Question 11

How much force is required to lift the weights?

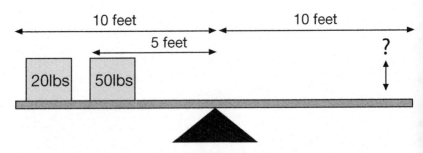

A	B	C	D
20 lbs	70 lbs	35 lbs	45 lbs

Question 12

Which post is carrying the greatest load?

Answer

Question 13

What would happen to a balloon full of air if you were to place it 15 feet below a water surface?

A – The volume of the balloon would increase

B – The volume of the balloon would stay the same

C – The balloon would explode

D – The volume of the balloon would decrease

Answer

Question 14

Which of the following statements will increase the mechanical advantage of this inclined plane?

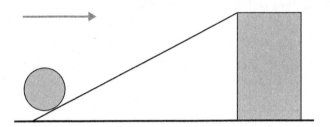

A – Shorten the length of the ramp

B – Make the ramp longer

C – Increase the slope of the ramp

D - Lessen the force acting at the arrow

Answer

Question 15

Which of the shelves can carry the heaviest load?

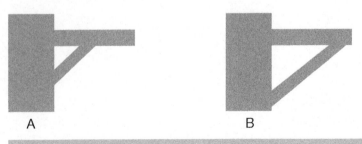

A   B

A	B	C
Shelf A	Shelf B	Both the same

Question 16

How much force is required to move the following weight?

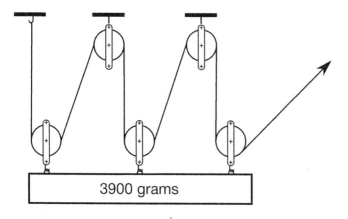

A	B	C	D
65 grams	1950 grams	650 grams	4000 grams

Question 17

How much weight is required to hold the load?

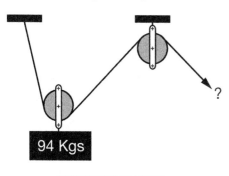

Answer

Question 18

A valve is used to perform which of the following tasks?

A – Control the flow of a liquid.

B – Increase the temperature of a liquid.

C – Facilitate the evaporation of a liquid.

D – Decrease the density of a liquid.

Answer

Question 19

At what point would you need to place weight X in order for the scales to balance?

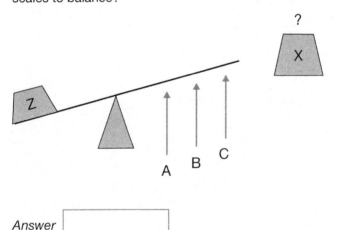

Answer

Question 20

Approximately how much force is required in order to lift the load?

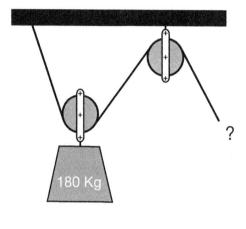

180 Kg

?

Answer

ANSWERS TO MECHANICAL COMPREHENSION

Q1. A

EXPLANATION = load A weighs less because the scales at point A are higher than they are for point B.

Q2. C

EXPLANATION = the beam will balance at point C. The bigger load needs to be balanced by the point of the beam. Only point C will balance the beam.

Q3. A = post A

EXPLANATION = post A is carrying the greatest load, because the load is positioned closer to post A as opposed to post B.

Q4. A

EXPLANATION = container A would register the highest reading.

Q5. A = clockwise

EXPLANATION = if cog A turns anti-clockwise, that means the cogs touching cog A will be rotated clockwise, and those touching them would go anti-clockwise and so forth. Therefore cog D will turn clockwise.

Q6. B = A

EXPLANATION = when answering questions where there is a single pulley system, if the pulley is fixed, as in A, then the force required to lift the weight is the same as the weight, i.e. 45kg. However, where the pulley system is not fixed and it moves with the weight (as is the case with pulley system B) then the weight required to lift it is half the weight. This means that the weight required to lift B is 22.5kg. The answer to the question is therefore B, as pulley system A requires the most weight to lift it.

Q7. A = 105 rpm

EXPLANATION = Wheel A is three times greater in diameter than wheel B, meaning that each revolution of A will lead to 3 times the revolution of B. Therefore, if wheel A rotates at 35 rpm, B will rotate at 35rpm × 3 = 105 rpm.

Q8. A = pole 1

EXPLANATION = pole 2 has the most pressure, because it is holding the whole weight of the object, whereas pole 1 is only holding half of the objects weight.

Q9. 2250 ft. lb.

EXPLANATION = 750 x 3 = 2250 ft. lb.

Q10. B = 1350 rpm

EXPLANATION = the large wheel rotates three times less than the smaller wheel. So, if the larger wheel is rotating at 450 rpm, this means that the smaller wheel must be rotating at a rate of three times faster. So, 450 x 3 = 1350 rpm.

Q11. D = 45 lbs

EXPLANATION =   f = (20 x 10) + (50 x 5) ÷ 10

f = (200) + (250) ÷ 10

f = 450 ÷ 10 = 45 lbs.

Q12. B

EXPLANATION = post B is carrying the heaviest load, because its surface area is larger.

Q13. D = the volume of the balloon would decrease

EXPLANATION = if you were to place a balloon full of air 15 feet under a water surface, the volume of the balloon would decrease. The pressure on the balloon from the water would press inwards, and this would cause the balloon to shrink in size, subsequently decreasing the volume of the balloon.

Q14. B = make the ramp longer

EXPLANATION = you need to make the ramp longer in order to increase the mechanical advantage of this inclined plane.

Q15. B = shelf B

EXPLANATION = the shelf that can carry the most weight is shelf B. The bar holding the shelf up is positioned better in order to hold more weight. Shelf A has the diagonal bar positioned in the middle, and therefore placing a lot of weight on the shelf would cause it to collapse on the right side.

Q16. C = 650 grams

EXPLANATION = the weight of the object is 3900 grams. There are 6 sections (parts of the rope) supporting the weight. So, you need to divide 3900 by 6 to generate your answer. $3900 \div 6 = 650$ grams.

Q17. 47 kilograms

EXPLANATION = $94 \div 2$ (supporting ropes) = 47 kilograms.

Q18. A = Control the flow of a liquid

EXPLANATION = a valve is used to control the flow of a liquid.

Q19. A

EXPLANATION = in order for the scales to balance, the weight would need to be positioned at point A.

Q20. 90 kilograms

EXPLANATION = $180 \div 2$ (supporting ropes) = 90 kilograms.

ELECTRICAL COMPREHENSION TEST

During the aptitude tests, you will be required to sit an Electrical Comprehension assessment. The test itself is designed to assess your ability to work with different electrical concepts. On the following pages, I have provided you with a number of sample questions to help you prepare for the tests. Work through them as quickly as possible but remember to go back through and check the questions you got wrong; and more importantly, make sure you understand how the correct answers are reached.

If you struggle to understand the concepts of electrical circuits and terminology, then you may wish to purchase our Electrical Comprehension Tests guide to further aid you during this section. This guide can be obtained via www.how2become.com or www.amazon.co.uk.

Mechanical Comprehension Sample Exercise

ELECTRICAL COMPREHENSION

EXAMPLE 1

It is important that you are able to differentiate between series circuits, and parallel circuits. To distinguish between these two types of circuits, you should remember the following points:

- If there are no branches, then it is a **series** circuit;
- If there are branches, it is a **parallel** circuit.

Fairy lights

Series circuits can be described using the example of fairy lights. It is an electrical circuit in which the devices are connected end-to-end. It only has one path of flow.

Any break in the series of lights, results in no flow of electricity. In other words, if one light in the sequence breaks, the others will stop working.

Homes

Parallel circuits means more than one path of flow.

For example, in order to use multiple devices in your home, you use multiple paths of wiring that connects to an electrical circuit. This allows you to continue watching TV whilst turning off the lights.

ELECTRICAL COMPREHENSION

EXAMPLE 2

Electricity is a form of energy. You need to be fully aware of the dangers involved when using electrical components.

Below is a list of examples of ways in which you can be electrocuted if you are not careful when handling electricity:

• Pushing objects into plug sockets;

• Water touching an electrical compliance;

• Damaged wiring;

• Incorrect wiring;

• Overheated cables and plug sockets;

• Frayed cables.

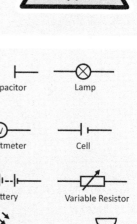

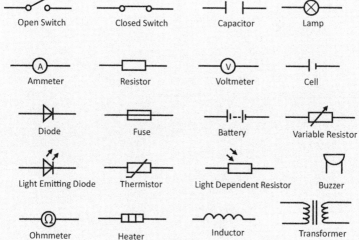

Open Switch	Closed Switch	Capacitor	Lamp
Ammeter	Resistor	Voltmeter	Cell
Diode	Fuse	Battery	Variable Resistor
Light Emitting Diode	Thermistor	Light Dependent Resistor	Buzzer
Ohmmeter	Heater	Inductor	Transformer

ELECTRICAL COMPREHENSION

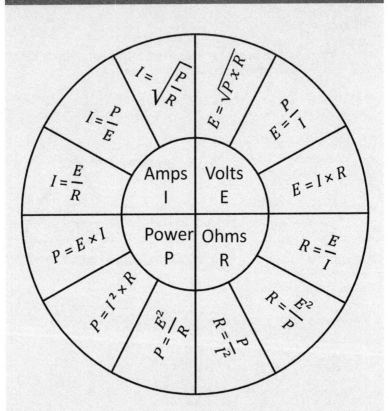

ELECTRICAL COMPREHENSION TEST

Question 1

Electrical power is measured in what?

A – Watts

B – Amps

C – Volts

D – Centimetres

Answer

Question 2

The basic particles that make up an atom are what?

A – Neutrons, protons and electrons

B – Protons, neutrons and particles

C – Protons and electrons

D – Mesons, neutrons and electrons

Answer

Question 3

Which of the following statements best describes Ohm's Law?

A – The relationship between voltage, current and resistance.

B – The total resistance in an electrical circuit.

C – E = MC2.

D – An equation.

Answer [   ]

Question 4

10 kilovolts is the equivalent to which of the following?

A – 10 millivolts

B – 1.0 volts

C – 1000 volts

D – 10000 volts

Answer [   ]

Question 5

Ohm's Law states that current is directly proportional to which of the following?

A – Resistance

B – Voltage

C – Temperature

D – Gas

Answer

Question 6

The unit of electrical potential or pressure is which of the following?

A – Watt

B – Amp

C – Volt

D – Current

Answer

Question 7

Removing the electrons from an atom would make the atom what?

A – Positively charged

B – Neutral

C – Negatively charged

D – A positive ion

Answer [   ]

Question 8

Current is measured in what?

A – Volts

B – Amps

C – Ohms

D – Watts

Answer [   ]

Question 9

Resistance is measured in what?

A – Volts

B – Amps

C – Ohms

D – Watts

Answer

Question 10

The ampere is a measure of what?

A – The power in a circuit.

B – The number of amps across a resistor.

C – The electrical pressure flowing in a circuit.

D – The number of electrons per second flowing in a circuit past a given point.

Answer

Question 11

What is the SI unit of capacitance?

A – Ohm

B – Farad

C – Watt

D – Amps

Answer [   ]

Question 12

Which of the following statements best describes the function of a capacitor?

A – Converts energy into sound.

B – Supplies the electrical charge.

C – Stores the electrical charge of the circuit.

D – A coil of wire which creates a magnetic field when current passes through.

E – Converts energy into light.

Answer [   ]

Question 13

In the following circuit, if bulb 1 is removed and the switch is closed, which bulbs will illuminate?

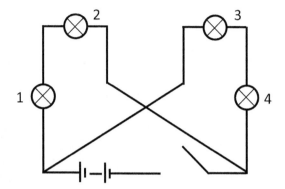

A – Bulb 4 will illuminate.

B – Bulbs 1, 2 and 4 will illuminate.

C – Bulbs 3 and 4 will illuminate.

D – Bulbs 1 and 4 will illuminate.

E – No bulbs will illuminate.

Answer

Question 14

An amplifier has an output of 2.15 V. If the gain is 320, calculate the input. Rounded to two decimal places.

A – 6.71 mV.

B – 6.27 mV.

C – 6.11 mV.

D – 6.72 mV.

Answer

Question 15

Identify the following electrical symbol.

Answer

Question 16

Identify the following electrical symbol.

Answer

Question 17

Identify the following electrical symbol.

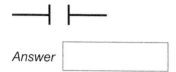

Answer

Question 18

Which two diagrams of the ammeters are NOT connected correctly? Circle two.

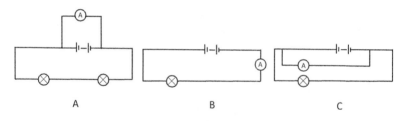

A	B	C
Diagram A	Diagram B	Diagram C

Question 19

35 kilovolts is the equivalent to which of the following?

A – 35 millivolts.

B – 3.4 volts.

C – 3000 volts.

D – 35,000 volts.

E – 350 millivolts.

Answer

Question 20

A current of 8.5 A passed through a circuit in 5 minutes. What is the quantity of electricity that is transferred?

A – 2970 C.

B – 2550 C.

C – 50 C.

D – 42.5 C.

Answer

ANSWERS TO ELECTRICAL COMPREHENSION

Q1. A

EXPLANATION = electrical power is measured using watts.

Q2. A

EXPLANATION = the three elements that make up an atom are protons, neutrons and electrons.

Q3. A

EXPLANATION = Ohm's law refers to the mathematical formula comprising the relationships found between the current, voltage and resistance within an electronic circuit.

Q4. D

EXPLANATION = a 'kilo' is equivalent to 1,000. So 10 kilovolts is equivalent to 10,000 volts.

Q5. B

EXPLANATION = Ohm's law states that current is directly proportional to the voltage.

Q6. C

EXPLANATION = the unit of electrical potential or pressure is volts.

Q7. D

EXPLANATION = removing the electrons from an atom would make the atom a positive ion.

Q8. B

EXPLANATION = current is measured in amps.

Q9. C

EXPLANATION = resistance is measured in ohms.

Q10. D

EXPLANATION = the ampere is a measure of the number of electrons per second flowing in a circuit past a given point.

Q11. B

EXPLANATION = the SI unit of capacitance is the farad.

Q12. C = stores the electrical charge of the circuit.

EXPLANATION = a capacitor is used to store the electrical charge of the circuit. It acts as a 'filter', blocking direct current (DC) signals, but permitting alternating current (AC) signals from running through the circuit.

Q13. C = Bulbs 3 and 4 will illuminate

EXPLANATION = only bulbs 3 and 4 will illuminate. If bulb 1 is removed, this will prevent bulb 2 from illuminating because they run on the same path. Bulbs 3 and 4 are on a different path of wiring, and therefore are not effected.

Q14. D = 6.72 mV

EXPLANATION = in order to work out the input, you should use the following method:

Output ÷ gain = 2.15 ÷ 320 = 0.00671875 x 1000 = 6.71875. To two decimal places = 6.72 mV.

Q15. Light emitting diode (LED)

EXPLANATION = the symbol represents a light emitting diode.

Q16. Thermistor

EXPLANATION = the symbol represents a thermistor.

Q17. Capacitor

EXPLANATION = the symbol represents a capacitor.

Q18. A + C

EXPLANATION = diagrams A and C are NOT connected correctly. Diagram B is the only diagram that is connected correctly.

Q19. D = 35,000 volts

EXPLANATION = a kilo is equivalent to 1000 volts. Therefore 35 kilovolts is equivalent to 35,000 volts.

Q20. B = 2550 C

EXPLANATION = in order to work out the electricity transferred, you should use the following method: 8.5 x 5 x 60 = 2550 C.

MEMORY TEST

During the aptitude selection tests, you will be required to under-take a memory test. The test is usually in two parts. During the first part of the test you will be required to view a sequence of letters. The letters will appear on a screen for a period of time. After that time, the sequence will disappear and you will then be required to answer questions relating to that sequence.

Memory Test Sample Exercise

Let's assume that the sequence of letters looks like the following. Please note that during the real test the letters may appear indi-vidually over a set period of time and not collectively as per below.

W	E	Q	X	R	E

Study the above sequence of letters for one minute only. Once the minute is up, cover the above sequence with your hand or a sheet of paper, and answer the following questions:

Question 1

How many letter E's were in the sequence?

Answer

Question 2

How many letters were there in between the letter W and the letter X?

Answer

Question 3

What letter was between the letter Q and the letter R?

Answer

Hopefully you managed to get the questions correct. Your ability to successfully pass this test will be dependent on how good your memory is. In order to improve your ability during this test, try the following sample exercises.

MEMORY TEST

Study the below sequence of letters for <u>one minute only</u>.
Once that minute is up, cover the sequence with your hand
or a sheet of paper and answer the following questions.

B	I	O	P	B	C

Question 1

How many letters were there in between the letter I and the letter C?

Answer

Question 2

How many letter P's were there in the sequence?

Answer

Question 3

What letter was in-between the letter O and the letter B?

Answer

Study the below sequence of letters for <u>one minute only</u>. Once that minute is up, cover the sequence with your hand or a sheet of paper and answer the following questions.

M	N	N	K	S	N

Question 4

What was the last letter in the sequence?

Answer

Question 5

How many letters were there in between the letter M and the letter S?

Answer

Question 6

What was the fourth letter in the sequence?

Answer

Study the below sequence of letters for <u>one minute only</u>. Once that minute is up, cover the sequence with your hand or a sheet of paper and answer the following questions.

X	a	C	C	p	A

Question 7

How many capital letters were there in the sequence?

Answer

Question 8

How many letters are between the letter X and the letter A?

Answer

Question 9

How many lower case letters (i.e. non-capital) were there in the sequence?

Answer

Study the below sequence of letters for <u>one minute only</u>. Once that minute is up, cover the sequence with your hand or a sheet of paper and answer the following questions.

e	E	e	V	E	o

Question 10

How many letter E's were in the sequence (capital or non-capital)?

Answer

Question 11

What letter comes fifth in the sequence?

Answer

Question 12

What letter comes last in the sequence?

Answer

Study the following grids for _10 seconds only_. Then turn the page and decide from the four options available which grid contains the collective group of coloured squares from the grids.

Question 13

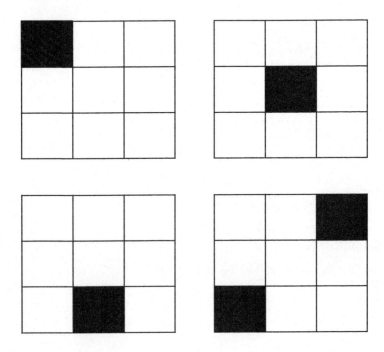

QUESTION 13 OPTIONS

A

B

C

D

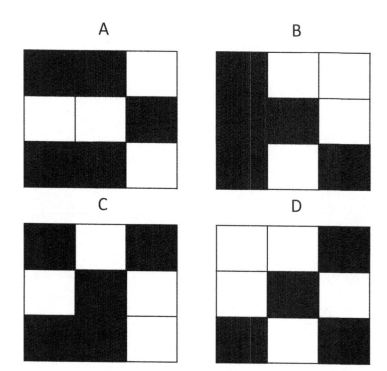

Answer

Study the following grids for 10 seconds only. Then turn the page and decide from the four options available which grid contains the collective group of coloured squares from the grids.

Question 14

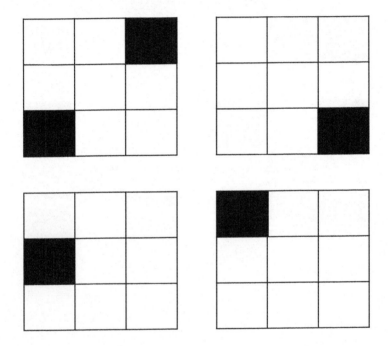

QUESTION 14 OPTIONS

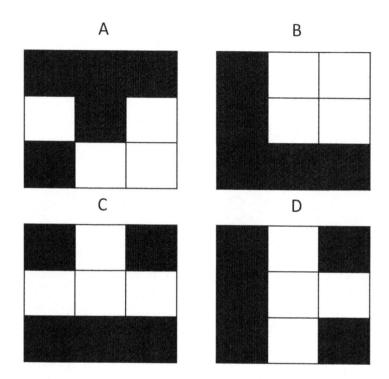

Answer

Study the following grids for 10 seconds only. Then turn the page and decide from the four options available which grid contains the collective group of coloured squares from the grids.

Question 15

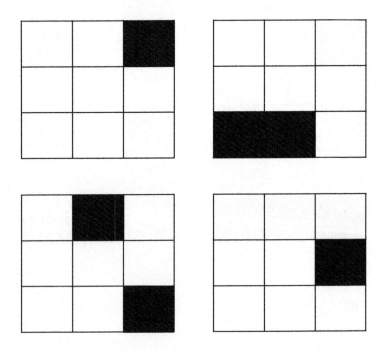

QUESTION 15 OPTIONS

A

B

C

D

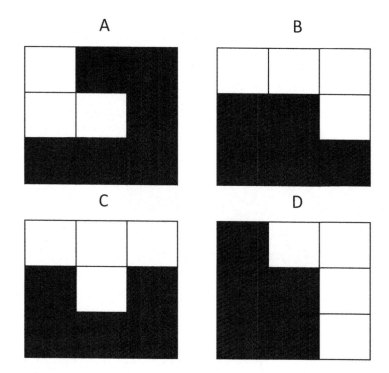

Answer

Study the following grids for 10 seconds only. Then turn the page and decide from the four options available which grid contains the collective group of coloured squares from the grids.

Question 16

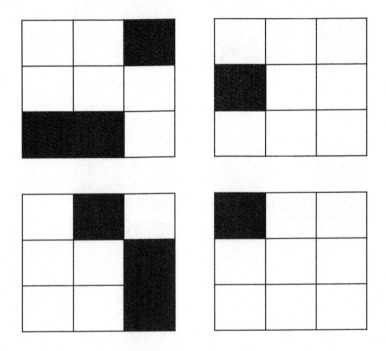

QUESTION 16 OPTIONS

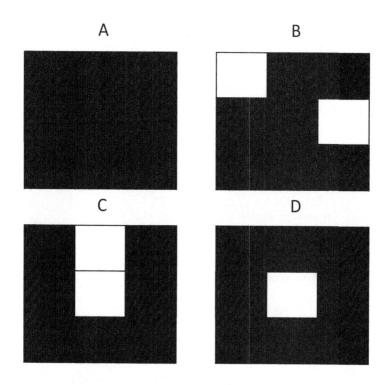

Answer

Study the following grids for 10 seconds only. Then turn the page and decide from the four options available which grid contains the collective group of coloured squares from the grids.

Question 17

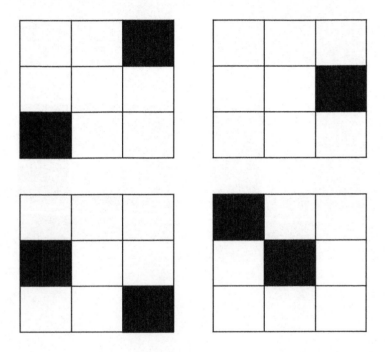

QUESTION 17 OPTIONS

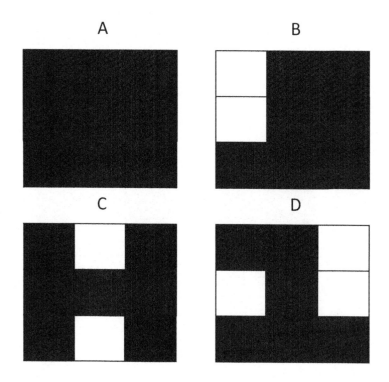

Answer

Study the following grids for 10 seconds only. Then turn the page and decide from the four options available which grid contains the collective group of coloured squares from the grids.

Question 18

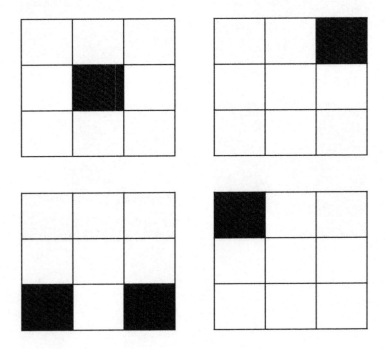

QUESTION 18 OPTIONS

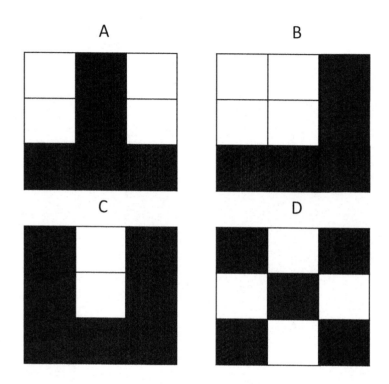

A

B

C

D

Answer

Study the following grids for 10 seconds only. Then turn the page and decide from the four options available which grid contains the collective group of coloured squares from the grids.

Question 19

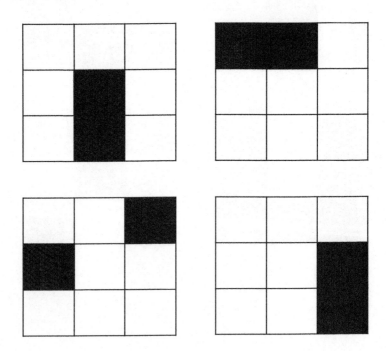

QUESTION 19 OPTIONS

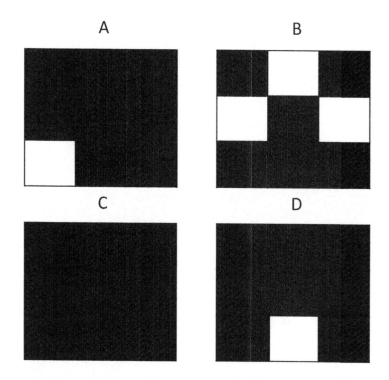

Answer

Study the following grids for 10 seconds only. Then turn the page and decide from the four options available which grid contains the collective group of coloured squares from the grids.

Question 20

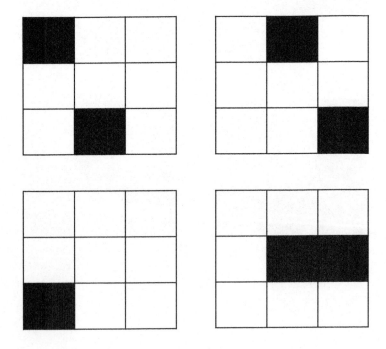

QUESTION 20 OPTIONS

A

B

C

D

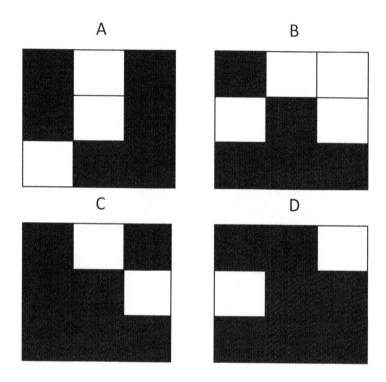

Answer

ANSWERS TO MEMORY TEST

Q1. 3

Q2. 1

Q3. P

Q4. N

Q5. 3

Q6. K

Q7. 4

Q8. 4

Q9. 2

Q10. 4

Q11. E

Q12. o

Q13. C

Q14. D

Q15. A

Q16. D

Q17. C

Q18. D

Q19. A

Q20. D

CHAPTER 6

*RAF Reserves
Interview*

During the RAF Reserves selection process, you will be required to sit a number of interviews depending on the role for which you are applying. For some of the more technical or demanding posts, you will be required to attend a specialist interview which will be held at an RAF base. These can last up to three days depending on the career. This is also an opportunity for you to see what the job is like and meet some of the people you would be expected to work with once you have passed your initial training.

The first interview will be held at your local Armed Forces Careers Officer and will be undertaken with a member of the RAF recruitment team. The duration of the interview will very much depend on your responses to the questions. However, you can expect the interview to last for approximately 30 minutes. The questions that you will be assessed against will normally be taken from the following areas:

- The reasons why you want to join the RAF Reserves;

- What choice of career you are most interested in, the reason for choosing that career and the skills you have to match the role;

- What information you already know about the RAF Reserves, their lifestyle and their training;

- Information relating to your hobbies and interests, including sporting/team activities;

- Any personal responsibilities that you currently have at home, in your education or at work;

- Information about your family and your partner and what they think about you joining;

- Information based around your initial application;

- Your experience of work and education;

- Your emotional stability and your maturity;

- Your drive and determination to succeed.

- Having a positive reaction to a disciplined environment and towards people in positions of higher authority.

Before I move on to a number of sample interview questions and responses, I want to explain a little bit about interview technique and how you can come across in a positive manner during the interview.

During my career in the Fire Service I sat on many interview panels assessing people who wanted to become a firefighter. As you can imagine, there were some good applicants and there were also some poor ones. Let me explain the difference between a good applicant and a poor one.

A Good Applicant...

A good applicant will demonstrate the following key characteristics:

- They are someone who has taken the time to fully prepare for the interview stage of the selection process;

- They will have researched both the organisation they are applying to join and the role for which they are applying. They may not know every detail about the organisation and the role, but it will be clear to the interviewers that they have made an effort to find out important facts and information;

- They will be well presented at the interview and convey the right amount of confidence;

- As soon as they walk into the interview room they will be polite and courteous, and they will sit down in the interview chair only when invited to do so;

- Throughout the interview they will sit upright in the chair and communicate in a positive manner;

- At the end of the interview they will ask positive questions about the job or the organisation, before shaking hands and leaving.

A Poor Applicant...

A poor applicant could be any combination of the following:

- They will be late for the interview or even forget to turn up at all;

- They will have made little effort to dress smart and they will have carried out little or no preparation;

- When asked questions about the job or the organisation, they will have little or no knowledge;

- Throughout the interview they will appear to be unenthusiastic about the whole process and will look as if they want the interview to be over as soon as possible;

- Whilst sat in the interview chair they will slouch and fidget. At the end of the interview they will try to ask clever questions that are intended to impress the panel. They may also ask questions about pay, or might even ask no questions at all.

Earlier on in the guide I made reference to a 'mock interview'. I strongly advise that you try out a mock interview before the real thing. You'll be amazed at how much your confidence will improve. All you need to do is get your parents or a friend to sit down with you and ask you the interview questions that are contained within this guide. Try to answer them as if you were at the real interview. The more mock interviews you try, the more confident you'll become.

Now let's take a look at a number of sample interview questions. Please note that these questions are not guaranteed to be the exact ones you'll hear during the real interview, but they are a great starting point in your preparation.

Use the sample responses that I have provided as a basis for your own preparation. Construct your answers based on your own opinions and experiences.

SAMPLE QUESTION 1

Why do you want to join the RAF Reserves?

You are almost guaranteed to hear this question during the selection interview, so there should be no reason why you can't answer it in a positive manner. Only you will know the real reason why you want to join, but consider the following benefits before you construct your response:

- A career in the RAF Reserves presents a challenge that is not available in the majority of other jobs;

- A career in the RAF Reserves will provide you with professional training and ongoing personal development;

- A career in the RAF Reserves allows you to live a normal life, with the same training benefits as full time employees, without spending frequent time away from home;

- A career in the RAF Reserves will offer you the chance to work in a highly professional organisation, which prides itself on high standards.

Try to display a good level of motivation when answering questions of this nature. The Royal Air Force is looking for people who want to become a professional member of their team, who understand their way of life. It should be your own decision to join the Royal Air Force, and you should be attracted to what this career has to offer. If you have been pushed into joining by your family, then you shouldn't be there! Below, I have provided you with a sample response to this question:

Sample Response:

'I have wanted to join the RAF Reserves for a couple of years now, and I have been working very hard to pass the selection process. Having studied the recruitment literature, and the RAF website, I am impressed by the professionalism and standards that the service sets for itself. I would like a career that is fulfilling, challenging and rewarding, and I believe that the RAF would provide all of these. During my research, I have spoken to serving members of the RAF Reserves and every single one of them had positive things to say about the role. The fact that I would be training in otherwise unreachable skills and furthering my education, whilst still living my normal life back at home, is just another example of why I want to join the Reserves. Over the last few years I have become more aware of my own skills and qualities, and I believe these would be very well suited to the RAF. I am someone who likes to take responsibility, and have demonstrated this on a number of occasions. For example, I was recently made Captain of my football team, a role which involves organising team trips and fixtures. I am also a good team player, and enjoy working with different groups of people who have had different experiences in their life. There is always something to learn, and I would love to be part of a service such as the RAF, where I would be continually learning new skills.

I have seriously considered the implications of joining the RAF Reserves, including the impact on my personal life and my social life. I know that there is a very real chance of me being called up to serve alongside full time troops in combat areas, and I am 100% prepared to fulfil my commitment to the service should this arise. I have the full support of my family and partner, and they have promised to help me achieve my goal of joining the RAF Reserves. While I know that the training will be hard, I am certain that I can pass with flying colours'.

SAMPLE QUESTION 2

What does your family think of you wanting to join the Royal Air Force?

What your family think about you wanting to join the RAF is very important, simply for the reason that you will need their support both during your training and during your career.

I can remember my parents being fully behind my decision to join the Armed Forces, and I'm very glad that they were. After about two weeks into my basic training, I started to feel a little homesick, just like any young man would after being away from home for a long period of time. I rang my Dad and discussed with him how I felt. After about five minutes talking, I felt perfectly fine and I no longer felt homesick. During that conversation, he reminded me how hard I had worked to get a place on the course, and that he and my Mum wanted me to succeed. For that reason alone, I was glad that I had the support of my parents.

With this in mind, it is important that you discuss your plan to join the Reserves with your parents or your guardian. If you have a partner, then you obviously need to discuss it with them too. If they have any concerns whatsoever, then I would advise that you take them along with you to the Careers Office, so that they can discuss these concerns with the trained recruitment staff. Make sure you have their full support, as you will need it at certain points during your career. If you are called up for duty, your family will need to be prepared for the fact that you'll be away for extended periods of time. Even when you aren't serving, you will frequently take 2 week training periods where you'll be away from home, so they need to be ready to deal with your absence.

Sample Response:

'Before I made my application, I discussed my choice of career with both my parents and my boyfriend. Initially they were apprehensive, but they could see how motivated and excited I was, as I had explained everything that my research had taught me about the service. I showed them the recruitment literature, and even took them around an RAF museum to help them get on board with my application.

I understand that it is important for them to support me during my application, and I now have their full backing. I've told them everything I know about the training and the conditions I will serve under. They are aware that the RAF Reserves have a brilliant reputation, and although they are wary of the fact that I could be called into duty at any time, and will spend periods of time training away from home, they are understanding and accepting of why I want to join'.

SAMPLE QUESTION 3

What grades did you achieve at school and how do you feel about them?

Questions that relate to your education are common during the initial RAF interview. In addition to this, the interviewers might also ask you questions that relate to which schools or educational establishments you attended.

This kind of question is designed to assess your attitude towards your grades, and how hard you worked at school. As you can imagine, your grades will generally reflect how hard you worked, and therefore you will need to be totally honest in your response. If you achieved very few educational qualifications, then you will need to explain what you intend to do about this in the future.

Despite leaving school with very few GCSEs, it was only later in my life that I really started to realise my academic potential. Whilst waiting for my service start date in the Armed Forces, I went back to college and embarked on a foundation course to improve my grades. If you already have the grades that you wanted from your education, then congratulations, this question will be much easier to answer.

Sample Response:

'To be totally honest, I didn't do as well as I had hoped. The reason for this was that I didn't work hard enough during the build up to the exams. I would put in some preparation, but I now realise I should have worked harder. In order to improve my grades, I have decided to embark on a foundation course at my local college, and I start this in a month's time. In the build up to the selection, I have been focusing hard on improving my academic ability, and I know that I can do well on the written tests.

I've certainly learnt from my lack of educational qualifications, and I can assure you that if I am successful, I will be working extremely hard to pass all of my exams, during both my basic training and my branch training'.

SAMPLE QUESTION 4

What responsibilities do you have either at work, school or at home?

If you are called up to duty with the RAF, or during your training periods, you will be responsible for a number of things. Apart from being responsible for the upkeep of your kit and equipment, you will also have additional responsibilities, such as cleaning, ironing and being punctual at all times.

Candidates who have had little or no experience whatsoever of such duties prior to joining, may find it difficult to cope with. If you are someone who has already held positions of responsibility prior to applying, then this will work in your favour. If you haven't, then now is the time to make a change. Start taking responsibility for household tasks, such as the washing and cleaning. Learn how to iron your own clothes, and take on a part-time/full-time job that requires you to be responsible for a specific role.

You may even decide to join a group or youth organisation such as the air cadets or scouts. Whatever you do, make sure you are responsible for carrying out set tasks and jobs, and that you carry out these jobs professionally and to the best of your ability.

Sample Response:

'I currently hold a few responsibilities both at home and in my part-time job. I'm responsible for cleaning the house once a week, and I usually do this on a Sunday before I go and play football for my local team. I'm the captain of my team, which means I have to arrange the fixtures, book the football ground and collect the kit at the end of the match, before washing and drying it for the following week's fixture.

I have just started a new job at my local supermarket, where I'm responsible for serving customers and making sure that stock levels are maintained. This involves cross checking current stock levels with required standards, and I have to report daily to my manager with any discrepancies, missing items or goods. Whilst serving customers, I'm responsible for ensuring I give them a good level of service, and I also have to check people for identification if they appear to be under the required age to purchase alcohol or cigarettes.

I enjoy taking on responsibility, as it gives me a sense of achievement. I understand that I will need to be responsible during my training, not only for the upkeep of my kit and equipment, but for ensuring that I am punctual and that I make the time to study hard for my exams'.

SAMPLE QUESTION 5

How do you think you will cope with the discipline, regimentation and routine in the RAF?

When you join the RAF, you will be joining a military organisation that has a considerable amount of set procedures, standards and discipline codes. These are there for very good reason. They ensure that the organisation runs at an optimum level. Without them, things would go wrong, and people could be injured or killed.

To some people, these aspects of RAF life will come as a shock. The recruitment staff will want to know that you are someone who can cope with these aspects if they are called into duty, and during the training.

Remember, they are investing time, effort and resources into your training, so they want to know that you can handle their way of life.

When answering this type of question, you need to demonstrate both your awareness of what RAF life involves, and a positive attitude towards the disciplined environment. Study the recruitment literature and visit the careers website to get a feel for the type of training you will be expected to undertake.

Sample Response:

'I believe I would cope with it very well. In the build up to the selection process, I have been trying to implement routine and discipline into my daily life. I've been getting up at 6am every weekday, and going on a 3 mile run. This will prepare me for the early starts that I'll encounter during training.

I've also been learning how to iron my own clothes, and I've been helping around the house with cleaning and washing, much to the surprise of my parents! I fully understand that if the RAF is to function as effectively as it does, it needs a disciplined workforce. Without discipline, things could go wrong.

Employees who do not carry out their duties professionally could endanger lives. For example, I would like to become a Reserve Aircraft Technician. If I did not carry out my job correctly, and failed to look after my tools and equipment, I would be failing in my duty.

I fully understand why discipline is required and believe I would cope with it well. I am prepared to be ready whenever the RAF need me, and will take on any task that I am given with maximum efficiency'.

SAMPLE QUESTION 6

Are you involved in any sporting activities and how do you keep yourself fit?

You can almost guarantee that you will be asked this question during the selection interview, so make sure that you have something positive to respond with.

When answering questions based around your own physical fitness and the type of sporting activities that you are involved in, you need to be honest; but bear in mind the following points:

- Although you don't have to be super fit to join the RAF Reserves, you do need to have a good level of physical fitness, so being fit when applying is obviously an advantage.

- The RAF prides themselves on their ability to work as an effective team unit. Those people who engage in active team sports are more likely to be competent team members. If you play a team sport, this will be a good thing to tell the interviewers. If you don't, then it might be a good idea to go out and join one!

Sample Response:

'Yes, I am. I currently play in my local netball team and have been doing so for a number of years now. Maintaining a good level of fitness is something I enjoy. In addition to my netball involvement, I also go running 3 times a week. I'm aware that during the initial RAF recruit training course I will be pushed to my limits, so I need to be prepared for that. I believe the fact that I play team sports will help me get through my training.

I enjoy playing in the netball team, because when we are losing, everyone pulls together and we work hard to try and win the game back. After matches, we all meet in the club bar for a drink and chat about the game. During our training sessions we always work on our weakest areas and look for ways to improve as a team. Keeping fit is important to me, and something that I want to continue with throughout my career. I have been working hard to pass the pre-joining fitness test, and have made sure that I can easily pass the minimum standard required'.

SAMPLE QUESTION 7

What do you think the qualities of a good team player are?

As you are already aware, the RAF prides itself on the ability to operate as an effective team. Therefore, having knowledge of how a team operates and the qualities required to become a competent team player is a significant advantage. During an earlier section of the guide, you will recall that I made reference to some of the most important qualities that are required to operate as an effective team player.

When responding to this type of question, it would be an advantage if you could back up your response with an example of where you have worked in a team before.

Sample Response:

'A good team player must have many different qualities including an ability to listen carefully. If you don't listen to instructions, then you can't complete the task properly. In addition to listening carefully, you must be able to communicate effectively with everyone in the team. This will include providing support for the other team members, and also listening to other people's suggestions on how a task can be achieved. You also

must be able to work with anyone in the team, regardless of their age, background, religion, sexual orientation, disability or appearance. You can't discriminate against anyone, and if you do, then there is no place for you within that team.

You should be focused on the team's goal and must not be distracted by any external factor. Putting the needs of the team first is paramount. Finally, a good team player must be flexible, and able to adapt to the changing requirements of the unit.

I already have some experience of working in a team, and I know how important it is to work hard at achieving the task. I have a part time job at weekends working in my local super-market, and every week we have a team briefing. During the team briefings, my manager will inform us of what jobs need to be carried out as a priority. During one particular meeting, he asked three of us to clear a fire escape that had become blocked with cardboard boxes, debris and rubbish. He also asked us to come up with a plan to prevent it from happening again. We quickly set about removing the rubbish, and I was responsible for arranging for a refuse collection company to dispose of the waste. We also had to work together to find ways of preventing the rubbish from being haphazardly dis-posed in the same way in the future. The team sat down to-gether and wrote out a memorandum for our manager that he could distribute to all staff. At the end of the job, we'd worked well to achieve the task and no more rubbish was ever thrown in the fire escape. My manager was very pleased with the job we had done'.

SAMPLE QUESTION 8

What do you do in your spare time?

With questions of this nature, the Royal Air Force recruitment staff are looking to see if you use your leisure time wisely. This will tell them a lot about your attitude and motivation. We all know that some people spend their spare time doing nothing, or watching TV and playing computer games.

When you join the RAF, you won't have much time to do nothing, so tell them that you are active and spend your time doing worthwhile things. For example, if you are involved in any sports, outdoor activities or belong to any youth organisations, then these are ideal things to incorporate into your answer. You may also be involved in voluntary work or charity work. Once again, such pastimes will work in your favour if mentioned during the interview.

If you currently do very little with your spare time, then now is a good time to make a lifestyle change. Embark on a fitness routine or join an activity club or organisation.

Sample Response:

'During my spare time I like to keep active, both physically and mentally. I enjoy visiting the gym three times a week, and I have a structured workout that I try to vary every few months, to keep my interest up. When I attend the gym, I like to work out using light weights, and I also enjoy using the indoor rower. I always try to beat my best time over a 2000 metre distance.

I'm also currently taking a weekly evening class in Judo, which is one of my hobbies. I haven't achieved any grades yet, but I am taking my first one in a few weeks' time. I'm also a member of the local Air Cadet Force, which is an evening's commitment every week, and the occasional weekend. Of course, I know when it's time to relax, and usually do this by listening to music or playing snooker with my friends.

Overall, I would say that I'm quite an active person. I certainly don't like sitting around doing nothing, and that's why working in the Reserves would be perfect for me'.

SAMPLE QUESTION 9

Can you tell me about any achievements you have accomplished during your life?

Candidates who can demonstrate a history of achievement during the interview, are far more likely to pass the initial training course. Having achieved something in your life demonstrates that you have the ability to see things through to the end, which is crucial to a career in the RAF. It shows that you are a motivated person, who is determined to succeed.

When answering this question, try to think of examples where you have succeeded or achieved something relevant in your life. Some good examples of achievements are as follows:

- Winning a trophy with a football or hockey team;

- GCSEs and other educational qualifications;

- Duke of Edinburgh award;

- Being given responsibility at work or at school;

- Raising money for charity.

Obviously you will have your own achievements that you want to add in to your response, but below I have provided you with an example.

Once you have read it, try to think of occasions in your life where you have achieved something of importance.

Sample Response:

'Yes, I can. So far in my life I have achieved quite a few things that I am proud of. To begin with, I achieved good grades whilst at school, including a grade A in English. I worked very hard to achieve my grades and I'm proud of them. At weekends, I play rugby for a local team, and I've achieved a number of things with them. Apart from winning the league last year, we also held a charity match against the local police rugby team. We managed to raise £500 for a local charity, which was a great achievement.

More recently, I managed to achieve a huge increase in my fitness levels. I have been working very hard to improve my strength, fitness and overall stamina, in preparation for the RAF fitness tests. I've increased my scores on the bleep test, and can now swim 50 lengths of my local pool. When I started, I could hardly manage ten lengths!

I have learnt that you have to work hard in life if you want to achieve things, and I have a good positive attitude to hard work. My own personal motto is 'work hard and you'll be rewarded'.

SAMPLE QUESTION 10

Can you tell me what you have learnt about your chosen career?

Once again, this is an almost guaranteed question, so make sure you prepare fully for it. The only information you will need is either in the recruitment literature that you're provided with, or on the RAF careers website at www.raf.mod.uk.

For example, if you want to join the RAF as an Aircraft Technician, then visit the website and read up on the information available regarding this career. I would advise that you learn as much as possible about the training that you'll be required to undertake if you are successful. You should also ask your AFCO recruitment advisor for more information relating to your chosen career and training. They will be able to point you in the right direction.

On the following page, I have provided a sample response to this question, for somebody who is hoping to join the RAF as a Reserve Aircraft Technician. Use the example to create your own response, relevant to your chosen trade.

You may even wish to look at other avenues or research, to improve your knowledge and further demonstrate your determination to succeed. For example, if you wish to join the Reserves as a photographer, then why not buy a book relating to photographers? You could even embark on an evening class and start learning before you join!

Sample Response:

'I'm aware that up to one third of people who are employed by the RAF work in engineering. As an Aircraft Technician, it will be my responsibility to maintain the airframes and engines

of the RAF's aircraft. This will include the different mechanical components, hydraulics, gear boxes and flying controls to name just a few. It is important to ensure that the aircrafts are ready to fly at all times. Another important part of this job is the preparation of the aircraft before they take off and also checking them for damage when they return from flight. Finally, Aircraft Technicians are responsible for the complete overhaul of the aircraft after set periods of time. I also understand that my job wouldn't be 9 to 5 and I'd be required to work day shifts and night shifts. Being flexible is crucial to the role.

During my training I will start off as an Aircraft Maintenance Mechanic. This role will be vital to my development as I will get to learn from already serving Aircraft Technicians. At this initial stage of my training I will get to help the other members of the team replace aircraft components and also check the aircraft for damage after sorties and missions making sure they are ready to fly again. I'm also aware that the training for this RAF career earns you an Engineering Certificate at Level 3 and Key Skills at Level 2. Once I've completed my training and my NVQ Level 3 I will be awarded with an Advanced Apprenticeship in aeronautical engineering'.

FINAL INTERVIEW TIPS

Within this section of the guide, I will provide you with some final tips that will help you prepare for the RAF Reserve selection interviews. Remember that your success will very much depend on how prepared you are. Don't forget to work on your interview technique, carry out plenty of research and practice your responses to the interview questions.

• In the build up to the interview, carry out plenty of targeted preparation. Read your recruitment literature and spend time studying the RAF website. Ask the AFCO recruitment advisor to provide you with information about the training you'll undergo for both your chosen career and also your initial training;

• Work on your interview technique and make sure you try out at least one mock interview. This involves getting your family or friends to sit you down and ask you the interview questions that are contained within this guide;

• When you receive your date for the interview make sure you turn up on time. Check your travel and parking arrangements the day before your interview. The last thing you need is to be late for your interview!

• Think carefully about what you are going to wear for the interview. I am not saying that you should go out and buy an expensive suit but I do recommend you make an effort to dress smartly. Having said that, if you do decide to wear a smart suit or formal outfit, make sure it is clean and pressed. You can still look scruffy in a suit. Don't attend the interview unwashed, dirty or fresh from the building site!

• When you walk into the interview room, stand up straight with your shoulders back. Project an image of confidence and be polite, courteous and respectful to the interviewer at all times. Don't sit down in the interview chair until invited to do so. Waiting until you are asked will display good manners;

- Whilst you are in the interview chair, sit upright with your hands resting on your knees, palms facing downwards. It is OK to use your hands expressively, but don't overdo it;

- Don't slouch in the chair. At the end of each question adjust your position;

- Whilst responding to the interview questions make sure you speak up and be positive. You will need to demonstrate a level of motivation and enthusiasm during the interview;

- Go the extra mile and learn a little bit about the RAF's history. When the panel ask you, "What can you tell us about the Royal Air Force?" you will be able to demonstrate that you have made an effort to look into their history as well as their modern day activities;

- Ask positive questions at the end of the interview. Don't ask questions such as "How much leave will I get?" or "How often do I get paid?"

- If you are unsure about a question try not to waffle. If you do not know the answer, then it is OK to say so. Move on to the next question and put it behind you;

- Finally, believe in yourself and be confident.

After you have taken your interview, you will face a short wait whilst the RAF Reserves come to a decision on your application. If you have been successful, then congratulations. You can now move onto the next stage.

Your acceptance letter or email will invite you to attend a health assessment at an undisclosed location. This is a test that will examine your general medical wellbeing, but will be largely dependent upon the role in the Reserves that you are applying for. You should check with your careers office, or contact the Reserves, for more information on the exact physical requirements on the role.

In the next section, we'll look at the Fitness Tests, and how you can prepare for them.

CHAPTER 7

How To Get RAF Reserve Fit

Within this chapter, I have provided you with a number of exercises and tips that will assist you during your preparation for the Fitness Tests. At the time of publication, the test consists of a 1.5 mile run in a time of 12 minutes and 12 seconds for men and 14 minutes and 35 seconds for women. It will be carried out at either your local Armed Forces Careers Office or alternatively, a gymnasium.

Your preparation for passing the RAF Reserve selection process should include a structured fitness training programme. Do not make the mistake of solely working on your academic ability. If I was going through RAF selection right now, then I would mix up my academic studies and my knowledge of the RAF study with a proper structured fitness training programme. For example, if I had scheduled in 60 minutes AST preparation on a particular weekday evening, I would most probably go for a 3 mile run immediately after my AST work. This would allow me to free my mind from the high concentration levels I would have endured during my study.

In addition to improving your physical fitness levels, I also advise that you keep an eye on your diet and try to eat healthy foods and drink plenty of water. This will all go a long way to helping you improve your general well-being and ultimately improve your concentration levels. As with any form of exercise you should consult your doctor first.

WARNING: Ensure you take advice from a competent fitness trainer in relation to the correct execution of any of the exercises contained within this guide. You may find that the technique for carrying out the exercises contained within this guide differs from the requirements of the RAF.

PLANNING YOUR WORKOUTS AND PREPARING FOR THE PRE-JOINING FITNESS TEST

The key to a successful fitness preparation strategy is variety and continuous improvement. When you commence your fitness programme you should be highly motivated. The hard part will come a couple of weeks into your fitness programme when your rate of improvement decreases. It is at this point that you must vary your exercise routine in order to ensure that you stay on the right track, so that you don't lose interest. The reason why most people give up on their fitness regime is mainly due to a lack of proper preparation. Preparation is key to your success, and it is essential that you plan your workouts effectively.

Members of the Armed Forces are required to maintain high fitness levels. However, some branches of the Armed Forces require a higher standard than others, and your fitness training programme should reflect this. For example, a candidate who is applying to join the Royal Marines or the Parachute Regiment would concentrate a lot more on their fitness preparation than somebody who was applying to join the RAF Reserves. Work hard to pass the fitness test, but do not spend hours and hours at the gym or out running. Read on for some great ways to not only pass the Pre-Joining Fitness Test, but also to stay RAF fit all year round.

PERFORM A SELF-ASSESSMENT

The first step is to conduct a 'self-fitness test'. This should involve the following three areas:

-   A 1.5 mile run in the fastest time possible;

-   As many sit ups as possible in two minutes;

-   As many press ups as possible in two minutes;

These tests will be very easy to perform, and you will not need to attend a gym in order to carry them out. However, the 1.5 mile run that forms part of the fitness tests is usually carried out on a treadmill. Running on a treadmill requires a different technique to running on a road. Whilst not essential, I would recommend you try running on a treadmill prior to the actual test, so that you can become familiar with the technique required.

Once you have done all 3 tests, you should write down your results and keep them safe somewhere. After 2 weeks of following your new fitness regime, do all 3 tests again and check your results against the previous week's results. This is a great way to monitor your performance and progression, and will help you to stay motivated and focused on your goals.

KEEP AN EYE ON WHAT YOU EAT AND DRINK

Before we get started with stretching and targeted exercises, I would also recommend that you write down everything that you eat and drink for a whole week. You must include tea, water, milk, biscuits – anything and everything you digest.

You will soon begin to realise how much you are eating, and will notice areas in which you can make some changes. For example, if you are taking sugar with your tea, then why not try reducing or removing it altogether? If you do, then you will soon notice the difference. You are about to embark on a fitness training routine, and therefore you will need to fill your body with the right type of fuel. This includes both food and drink. Let's get one thing straight from the offset – if you fill your body with rubbish, then your fitness performance is likely to be on par with rubbish. If you fill it with the right nutrients and vitamins, then you will perform far more effectively.

When I was 26 years old, I decided to do my own version of the ironman challenge for a local charity. I swam 2 miles, then ran a marathon, before finally completing a 120 mile cycle! The end result was that I managed to raise over £10,000 for a children's hospice in Kent. In the six months prior to the challenge I trained very hard, but I also put just as much effort into what I ate and drank. This would prove crucial to my success.

During your fitness training programme, I recommend that you totally avoid high calorie foods, such as chips, burgers, chocolates, sweets, fizzy drinks and alcohol. Replace these with fruit, vegetables, pasta, rice, chicken and fish. You also need to make sure that you drink plenty of water throughout the day, in order to keep yourself fully hydrated. This will help to keep your concentration levels up, which you will need for the fitness tests. Many people will use vitamin supplements and energy enhancing drinks to do this. It is my opinion that you don't need any of these. Providing you drink plenty of water, and stick to a balanced diet which includes the right vitamins and nutrients, you will be in better mental and physical shape than anyone who is using 'quick fixes' to get ahead.

It is important that you start to look for opportunities to improve your fitness and well-being right from the offset.

YOU DON'T NEED TO LIFT HEAVY WEIGHTS IN ORDER TO PASS THE FITNESS TESTS

When I applied to join the Fire Service the physical tests were rigorous, demanding and extremely difficult to pass. As part of the assessment, I was required to bench press 50kg, 20 times within 60 seconds. It is my strong belief that you do not need to lift heavy weights in order to pass the fitness tests. In fact, I would go as far as to say that you don't need to lift any weights at all, other than your own body weight whilst doing press ups. If you do decide to lift weights, then you will be better off including some form of light weight work, which is specifically targeted at increasing stamina, strength and endurance. Instead of performing bench presses, replace them with press ups. Instead of performing heavy lateral pull down exercises, replace them with pull ups which only utilise your own body weight.

Within this chapter, you'll find a whole range of great exercise, most of which can be carried out without attending a gym.

ONE STEP AT A TIME

Only you will know how fit you are. The first thing that I would advise you to do, is to write down all of the areas which you believe you need to improve on. For example, if after carrying out your 3 self-fitness tests you realise you are going to struggle with running, then embark on a structured running programme which is designed to gradually improve your performance.

The key to making improvements is to do it gradually, taking one step at a time. Try to set yourself small goals. When you carry out your initial 'self-fitness test', you may find that you can only achieve a few press ups and sit ups. Instead of focusing on a higher target of 50 press ups within 2 minutes, break down your goals into easy-to-achieve stepping stones. For example, by the end of the first week aim to do an additional 10 press ups and sit ups. Then, add another 10 to the second week's target and so forth. One of the biggest problems that many people encounter when starting a fitness regime is that they become bored very quickly. This then leads to a lack of motivation and desire, and soon the fitness programme stops. Change your exercise routine often in order to maintain your interest levels. Instead of running every day, try swimming or indoor rowing. This will keep your interest and motivational levels high and it will also work other muscle groups that running cannot affect.

STRETCHING

How many people stretch before carrying out any form of exercise? Very few people, is the correct answer. Not only is it irresponsible, but it is also placing yourself at high risk of injury. The last thing you need is an injury, especially after the amount of hard work you will be putting in to successfully pass the selection process. Before I commence with the exercises, let's take a look at a few warm up stretches. Make sure you stretch fully before carrying out any exercise. It is also very important to check with your GP that you are medically fit to carry out any form of physical exercise.

The warm-up calf stretch

To perform this stretch effectively, you should start off by facing a wall whilst standing upright. Your right foot should be close to the wall, and your right knee should be bent. Now, place your hands flat against the wall and at a height that is level with your shoulders. Stretch your left leg out far behind you, without lifting your toes or heel off the floor, and then lean towards the wall.

Once you have performed this stretch for 25 seconds, switch legs and carry out the same procedure for the left leg. As with all exercises contained within this guide, stop if you feel any pain or discomfort.

Stretching the shoulder muscles

To begin with, stand your feet slightly apart, and your knees only slightly bent. Now, hold your arms right out in front of you, with your palms away from you and your finger pointing skywards. Now, place your right palm on the back of your left hand and use it to push the left hand further away from you. If you are performing this exercise correctly then you will feel the muscles in your shoulder stretching. Hold for 10 seconds before switching sides.

Stretching the quad muscles (front of the thigh)

Before you carry out any form of running, it is imperative that you stretch your leg muscles. As you are already aware, as part of the fitness test you are required to run a set distance in a set period of time. It is very important that you stretch fully before this test, and your instructor should take you through a number of stretching exercises before you begin your workouts.

To begin with, stand with your left hand pressed against the back of a wall or firm surface. Bend your left knee slightly, and bring your right heel up to your bottom whilst grasping your foot with your right hand. Your back should be straight, and your shoulders, hips and knees should all be in line at all times during the exercise. Hold for 25 seconds before switching legs.

Stretching the hamstring muscles (back of the thigh)

It is very easy to injure your hamstring muscles when working in the RAF Reserves, especially with all of the running you'll be doing during your initial basic training. Therefore, you must get into the routine of stretching out the hamstring muscles before every training session.

To perform this exercise correctly, stand up straight and place your right foot onto a table or other firm surface, so that your leg is almost parallel to the floor. Keep your left leg straight, and your foot at a right angle to your leg. Start to slowly move your hands down your right leg towards your ankle, until you feel tension on the underside of your thigh. When you feel this tension, you know that you are starting to stretch the hamstring muscles. Hold for 25 seconds before switching legs.

I have only covered a small number of stretching exercises within this section; however, it is crucial that you stretch out fully in all areas, before carrying out any of the following exercises. Remember to obtain professional advice before carrying out any type of exercise.

RUNNING

One of the best ways to prepare for the fitness tests is to embark on a structured running programme. You do not need to run extreme distances in order to gain from this type of exercise. As part of the fitness tests, you will be required to run 1.5 miles in a set period of time. Don't settle for the minimum standard, but instead keep pushing yourself and improving your stamina/fitness levels. Towards the end of this section, I have provided you with a number of weekly training programmes for you to follow.

Tips for Running

-   As with any exercise, you should consult a doctor before taking part, to make sure that you are medically fit;

Top Tips

-   It is certainly worth investing in a pair of comfortable running shoes, which serve the purpose of your intended training programme.
    Your local sports shop will be able to advise you on the types that are best for you. You don't have to spend a fortune to buy a good pair of running shoes;

-   It is a good idea to invest in a 'high visibility' jacket or coat, so that you can be seen by fast moving traffic, if you intend to run on or near the road;

-   Make sure you carry out at least 5 whole minutes of stretching exercises, not only before, but also after your running programme. This will help to prevent injury.

-   Whilst you shouldn't run on a full stomach, it is also not good to run on an empty one either. A great food to eat approximately 30 minutes before a run is a banana. This is great for giving you energy;

-   Drink plenty of water throughout the day. Drink at least 1.5 litres each day in total. This will keep you hydrated and help to prevent muscle cramp;

-   Don't overdo it. If you feel any pain or discomfort then stop and seek medical advice;

-   When preparing for the RAF selection process, use your exercise time as a break from your studies. For example, if you have been practising aptitude tests for an hour, why not take a break and go running? When you return from your run, you can then concentrate on your studies, feeling refreshed.

PRESS-UPS

Whilst running is a great way to improve your overall fitness, you will also need to carry out exercises that focus on improving your upper body strength. These exercises will help you to prepare for the RAF's basic training course.

The great thing about press-ups is that you don't have to attend a gym to perform them. However, you must ensure that you can do them correctly, otherwise injury can occur. You only need to spend 5 minutes every day on  press-ups, either after you go running or even before. If you are not used to doing press-ups, then start slowly and aim to carry out at least 10.

Even if you struggle to do just 10, after a few days practice of these you'll soon be up to 20+.

How to Perform this Exercise

Step 1:

To begin with, lie on a mat or even surface. Your hands should be shoulder width apart. Fully extend the arms.

Step 2:

Gradually lower your body until the elbows reach 90°. Do not rush the movement as you may cause injury.

Step 3:

Once your elbows reach 90°, slowly return to the starting position with your arms fully extended.

The press up action should be a continuous movement with no rest. However, it is important that the exercise is as smooth as possible, and there should be no jolting or sudden movements. Try to complete as many press ups as possible, and always keep a record of how many you do. This will keep your focus, and help maintain your motivation levels.

SIT-UPS

Sit-ups are great for building the core stomach muscles. Strong abdominal muscles are important for lifting equipment, something which is integral to many roles in the RAF Reserves.

How to Perform this Exercise:

Step 1:

At the commencement of the exercise, lie flat on your back with your knees bent at a 45° angle, with your feet together.

Step 2:

Your hands can either be crossed on your chest, by your sides or cupped behind your ears as indicated in the diagram below.

Step 3:

Without moving your lower body, curl your upper torso upwards and in towards your knees, until your shoulder blades are as high off the ground as possible.

Step 4:

As you reach the highest point, tighten your abdominal muscles for a brief second. This will allow you to get the most out of the exercise.

Step 5:

Now slowly start to lower yourself back to the starting position. You should be aiming to work up to at least 50 effective sit-ups within a two minute period. You will be amazed at how quickly this can be achieved and you will soon begin to notice your stomach muscles developing.

SQUATS

Squats are a great exercise for working the leg muscles. They are the perfect exercise in your preparation, as they will develop the leg muscles used for running.

How to Perform this Exercise:

Step 1:

At the commencement of the exercise, stand up straight with your arms at your sides. Concentrate on keeping your feet shoulder-width apart and your head up.

Step 2:

Do not look downwards at any point during the exercise.
You will see from the diagram below that the person has their lower back slightly arched. They are also holding light weights which can add to the intensity of the exercise.

Step 3:

As you come back up to a standing position, push down through your heels which will allow you to maintain your balance. Repeat the exercise 15 to 20 times.

LUNGES

The lunge exercise is another great addition to the range of exercises that require no attendance at the gym, and they also fit perfectly into the role of an RAF Airman/Airwoman. This is because they concentrate on building the necessary core muscles to perform the demanding tasks of the job, such as bending down and picking up items of equipment.

How to Perform this Exercise:

Step 1:

To begin with, stand with your back straight and your feet together.

Step 2:

Next, take a big step forward as illustrated in the diagram, making sure you inhale as you bend.

Step 3:

Bend the front knee no more than 90 degrees so as to avoid injury. Keep your back straight and lower the back knee as close to the floor as possible. Your front knee should be lined up over your ankle and your back thigh should be in line with your back.

Step 4:

To complete the exercise, exhale and push down against your front heel, squeezing your buttocks tight as you rise back to a starting position. Try to repeat the exercise 15 to 20 times before switching sides.

TRICEP DIPS

Tricep dips are brilliant at building the muscles in the rear of the arm. The triceps are a core muscle for upper body strength, and therefore it's important to spend time developing it. Once again, you do not have to attend a gym to work on this.

How to Perform this Exercise:

Step 1:

Place your hands shoulder width apart, on a bench or immovable object as the diagram illustrates.

Step 2:

Lower your body until your elbows are at an angle of 90 degrees.

Step 3:

Push back up so that the body returns to its starting position, breathing out on the way up. Ensure that your back remains close to the bench or object throughout the movement.

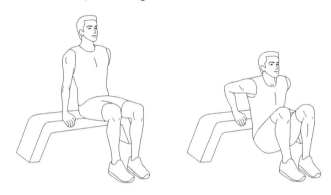

SWIMMING

Another fantastic way to improve your upper body and overall fitness is to go swimming. If you have access to a swimming pool, and you can swim, then this is a brilliant way to improve your fitness and especially your upper body strength.

If you are not a great swimmer you can start off with short distances and gradually build up your swimming strength and stamina.

Breaststroke is sufficient for building good upper body strength providing you put the effort into swimming an effective number of lengths. If you can swim 10 lengths of a 25-metre pool, then this is a good base to start from. You will soon find that you can increase this number easily, providing that you carry on swimming every week. Try running to your local swimming pool if it is not too far away, swimming 20 lengths of breaststroke, and then running back home. This is a great way to combine your fitness activity and prevent yourself from becoming bored with your training programme.

THE MULTI STAGE FITNESS TEST OR 'BLEEP TEST'

A great way to build endurance and stamina is by training with the multi stage fitness test or 'bleep test' as it is otherwise called. Once again, if you are applying to join the RAF Regiment, then the bleep test forms part of the fitness assessment. The multi stage fitness test is used by sports coaches and trainers to estimate an athlete's VO2 Max (maximum oxygen uptake). The test is especially useful for players of sports like football, hockey or rugby. You will most certainly have to carry out the test during your initial RAF basic training. The test itself can be obtained through various websites on the internet and it is great for building your endurance and stamina levels.

TRAINING PROGRAMMES

I believe that it is very important to add some form of 'structure' to your training programme. Apart from keeping you focused and motivated, it will also allow you to measure your results.

If I was going through the selection process right now, I would get myself a small notebook and pencil and keep a check of my times, distances, repetitions and exercises. I would try to improve on each area as each week passes. In order to help you add some form of structure to your training regime, I have provided you with four sample training programmes based on different intensities.

Before you carry out any form of exercise make sure you consult your doctor to ensure you are fit and healthy. Start off slowly and gradually increase the pace and intensity of your exercises.

Training programme 1

Day 1	Day 2	Day 3	Day 4	Day 5	Day 6 + 7
1.5 mile run (best effort) Record and keep results	3 mile run	Swimming (500 metres) or indoor rowing for 2000 metres	3 mile run	Swimming (500 metres) or indoor rowing for 2000 metres	Rest Day
50 sit ups and 50 press ups or as many as possible	50 sit ups and 50 press ups or as many as possible	10 mile cycle ride	50 sit ups and 50 press ups or as many as possible	50 sit ups and 50 press ups or as many as possible	Rest Day
50 sit ups and 50 press ups or as many as possible	50 sit ups and 50 press ups or as many as possible	10 mile cycle ride	50 sit ups and 50 press ups or as many as possible	50 sit ups and 50 press ups or as many as possible	Rest Day

Training programme 2

Day 1	Day 2	Day 3	Day 4	Day 5	Day 6 + 7
1.5 mile run (best effort) Record and keep results	Swimming (500 metres) or indoor rowing for 3000 metres	5 mile run	2 mile walk at a brisk pace followed by a 3 mile run	Swimming (1000 metres) or indoor rowing for 3000 metres	Rest Day
50 sit ups and 50 press ups or as many as possible	10 mile cycle ride	50 sit ups and 50 press ups or as many as possible		50 sit ups and 50 press ups or as many as possible	Rest Day
30 × Squat thrusts	20 × lunges each side and 30 × Star Jumps	Pull ups (as many as possible)	Pull ups (as many as possible)	30 × Squat thrusts 20 × lunges each side and 30 × Star Jumps	Rest Day

Training programme 3

Day 1	Day 2	Day 3	Day 4	Day 5	Day 6 + 7
1.5 mile run (best effort) Record and keep results	5 mile run	20 mile cycle ride	5 mile run	Swimming (1000 metres)	Rest Day
50 sit ups and 50 press ups or as many as possible	50 sit ups and 50 press ups or as many as possible	3 mile walk at a brisk pace	50 sit ups and 50 press ups or as many as possible	50 sit ups and 50 press ups or as many as possible	Rest Day
Swimming (500 metres)		30 × Squat thrusts 20 × lunges each side and 30 × Star Jumps		30 × Squat thrusts 20 × lunges each side and 30 × Star Jumps	Rest Day

Training programme 4

Day 1	Day 2	Day 3	Day 4	Day 5	Day 6 + 7
1.5 mile run (best effort) Record and keep results	Bleep test (best effort)	7 mile run	Swimming (1000 metres)	10 mile run	Rest Day
50 sit ups and 50 press ups or as many as possible	Pull ups (as many as possible) followed by 50 × Squat thrusts 25 × lunges each side and 50 × Star Jumps	70 sit ups and 70 press ups or as many as possible	Pull ups (as many as possible) followed by 50 × Squat thrusts 25 × lunges each side and 50 × Star Jumps	70 sit ups and 70 press ups or as many as possible	Rest Day
Swimming (1000 metres) Followed by a 3 mile brisk walk	20 mile cycle ride	30 × Squat thrusts 20 × lunges each side and 30 × Star Jumps	10 mile cycle ride	Swimming (500 metres) Followed by a 3 mile brisk walk	Rest Day

Tips for Staying with your Workout

The hardest part of your training programme will be sticking with it. In the final section of this chapter, I will provide you with some useful golden rules that will enable you to maintain your motivational levels in the build up to the RAF Fitness Test.

In order to stay with your workout for longer, try following these simple rules:

GOLDEN RULE 1 – WORK OUT OFTEN

Aim to train five days every week. Each training session should last between 20 minutes to a maximum of an hour. The quality of training is important, so don't go for heavy weights, but instead go for a lighter weight with a better technique. On days when you are feeling energetic, take advantage of this and do more!

Within this guide I have provided you with a number of 'simple to perform' exercises that are targeted at the core muscle groups required to pass the fitness tests, and also to prepare you for your RAF initial basic training course.

In between your study sessions, try carrying out these exercises at home or get yourself out on the road running or cycling. Use your study 'down time' effectively and wisely.

GOLDEN RULE 2 – MIX UP YOUR EXERCISES

Your exercise programme should include some elements of cardiovascular (running, bleep test, brisk walking, swimming and cycling), resistance training (weights or own body exercises such as press-ups and sit ups) and flexibility (stretching). Make sure that you always warm up and warm down.

If you are a member of a gym, then consider taking up a class such as Pilates. This type of exercise will teach you how to build core training into your exercise principles, and show you how to hit your abdominals in ways that are not possible with conventional sit-ups.

If you are a member of a gym, then a fantastic 'all round' exercise that I strongly recommend is rowing. Rowing will hit every major muscle group in your body and is also perfect for improving your stamina levels and cardiovascular fitness.

GOLDEN RULE 3 – EAT A HEALTHY AND BALANCED DIET

It is vitally important that you eat the right fuel. Don't fill your body with rubbish and then expect to train well. Think about what you are eating and drinking, including the quantity of food and drink. Keep a record of what you are digesting. You will become stronger and fitter more quickly if you eat little amounts of nutritious foods at short intervals.

GOLDEN RULE 4 – GET HELP

Try working with a personal trainer or someone else who is preparing for selection. They will ensure that you work hard and will help you to achieve your goals. The mere fact that they are there at your side will add an element of competition to your training sessions!

A consultation with a professional nutritionist will also help you to improve your eating habits and establish your individual food needs.

GOLDEN RULE 5 – FITNESS IS FOR LIFE

Working out and eating correctly are not short-term projects. These are things that should be as natural to us as brushing our teeth.

Make fitness a permanent part of your daily routine, and you'll lead a better and more fulfilling life!

CHAPTER 8

A Few
Final Words

You have now reached the end of the guide and will no doubt be ready to start preparing for the RAF Reserves selection process. Before you go and start your preparation, consider the following.

The majority of candidates who pass the RAF Reserves selection process have a number of common factors. These are as follows:

1. They believe in themselves.

The first factor is self-belief. Regardless of what anyone tells you, you can pass the selection process and you can achieve high scores. Just like any job of this nature, you have to be prepared to work hard in order to be successful. You will notice that the aptitude tests are extremely difficult, and therefore you will need to work hard to pass them. Ensure you have the self-belief to pass the selection process, by filling your mind with positive thoughts.

2. They prepare fully.

The second factor is preparation. Those people who achieve in life prepare fully for every eventuality and that is what you must do when you apply to become an RAF Reserve. Work hard and concentrate on your weaker areas. Within this guide I have spoken a lot about preparation. Identify the areas that you are weak on and go all out to improve them.

3. They persevere.

Perseverance is a fantastic word. Everybody comes across obstacles or setbacks in their life, but it is what you do about those setbacks that is important. If you fail at something, then consider 'why' you have failed. This will allow you to improve for next time and if you keep improving and trying, success will eventually follow. Apply this same method of thinking when you apply to join the Reserves.

4. They are self-motivated.

How much do you want to join the RAF Reserves? Do you want it, or do you really want it? When you apply to join the RAF you should want it more than anything in the world. Your levels of self-motivation will shine through when you walk into the AFCO and when you attend the interview. For the weeks and months leading up to the selection process, be as motivated you can and always keep your fitness levels up as this will serve to increase your levels of motivation.

Work hard, stay focused, and achieve anything you set your mind to.

Richard McMunn

Richard McMunn

Printed in Great Britain
by Amazon